Dedicated to

Students who wish to prepare themselves for the 21st century.

Teachers and parents who are keen to impart 21st-century skills.

Computational Thinking with Blockly Games

A step-by-step guide for young learners

(Colour version)

Dr Ashok Banerji

ISBN: 979 889 026 047-5

Contents

"Real education is that which enables one to stand on one's own legs."

Sw Vivekananda

Foreword

In today's technology-driven world, digital skills are essential for everyone. In addition to the basic literacies of reading, writing and arithmetic it is a necessity that every student be computer literate. Together it contributes to their Computational Thinking ability.

Digital computing devices produce desired output by running software designed and coded by programmers. Not everyone is expected to know to program in detail. However, a basic awareness of the logic, steps and processes helps make the best use of available technologies. Here, an analogy can be drawn with using a car. Not everyone is expected to be a car mechanic to drive a car. However, some knowledge about a car helps drive it for better performance.

Working with students for over 50 years I have realised that teaching the fundamental concepts of programming is something hard for new students. In this context, the book "Computational Thinking with Blockly Games" by Ashok Banerji is a welcome contribution. It is particularly so because it is targeted at young students who need to develop CT skills early in life.

The visual programming paradigm of Blockly is eminently suitable for this target group. Any computer program can be taken as a collection of blocks inside which appropriate codes exist. By manipulating the blocks one can create a program by building logic and sequence. Once such a structure is obtained, understanding coding and programming becomes easy.

Written as a step-by-step guide in simple language, this book will help children to learn coding through gameplay. The foundation knowledge will prepare them to develop programs and solve problems in any subject.

Dr A. M. Ghosh

Rtd. Professor and HOD Computer Science and Technology, Bengal Engineering and Science University (former IIEST) Shibpur

Vaiskhi, 14 April 2023

Preface

Many parents want to teach their children about coding but often do not know where to begin or what to cover. The idea for this book evolved to precisely address this need. It is meant for kids and anyone who wants to learn the basics of computer programming and Computational Thinking. Welcome to the world of Computational Thinking for young learners.

The book covers foundational problem-solving concepts through simple games, taking young students on a journey of thinking, planning, and solving problems.

The importance of teaching coding from the early school years is recognized by many countries. It is now mandatory under the new education policy of Govt. of India.

In order to adapt and absorb new material in changing fields, it is crucial for today's children not only to acquire knowledge but also to learn how to learn. This book aims to aid this process, promoting creativity and innovation.

Blockly Games have been adopted in this book as an enjoyable way to introduce computational thinking and programming concepts. The book follows a graded pedagogy with guided discovery, semi-guided lessons, and open-ended exploration.

By developing computational and digital skills, children can collaborate, create, and find relevance in nearly all subjects.

This book hopes to build a strong foundation in coding principles and welcomes any suggestions for improvement.

So, let's get started.

Dr. Ashok Banerji

Vaiskhi, 14th April 2023

Acknowledgements

I express acknowledgement to all the children who attended my training sessions. Interactions with them and watching their achievements motivated me to write this book.

Case studies of two students of class five over a year back would be instructive. I remember Daiwik Bhattacharjee and Aryan Chatterjee from Mumbai. Aryan programmed wonderful music compositions with the music module of Blockly Games because of his love of music. Daiwik displayed self-leaning capability. He learned JavaScript on his own just by watching the code displayed at the end of each game. He developed an interesting program in JavaScript in the last module of Blockly Games. Daiwik also tested the codes used in this book and evaluated the contents from the young learners' perspective.

Special thanks are expressed to Google Inc. for creating the open-source Blockly Games - a product of Google project to encourage 'tomorrow's programmers'. Certainly, it meets the objective very well to make the players ready with the foundation programming concepts and constructs. More importantly, we have found that it promotes Computational Thinking skills through playful challenges by solving different levels of the games.

I acknowledge the open-source flow diagramming tool, Dia available at https://wiki.gnome.org/Dia. Flow Diagrams have been drawn using this app. I will encourage students to use this application for drawing flowcharts.

Note for Teachers and Parents

The book is meant for

- Anyone from 8-108 years to expand their capacity.
- Persons interested in learning 21st century skills.
- Explorers who love solving puzzles and problems.
- Teachers and parents who wish to equip students with essential 21st century skills.

What will you learn?

- Learn the basics of computational logic.
- Playfully learn basic programming principles.
- Independently plan and act to solve problems.
- Implement solution using the available resources.

Prerequisites to use this book effectively.

- Students should be able to read and understand simple English.
- Have the determination and resilience to solve problems.
- Be able to think independently.
- Have the knowledge of using a computer, keyboard, and mouse.

The book is a basic course on Computational Thinking in three phases (a) Guided lessons (Chapter 1 to 14) (b) Semi guided lessons (Chapter 15 to 16) and (c) Exploratory lessons (Chapter 17 to 20).

Students should work persistently on their own. After completing the book, they will prove the following words of Swami Vivekananda:

"No one was ever really taught by another; each of us has to teach himself. The external teacher offers only the suggestion which rouses the internal teacher to work to understand things."

1. Getting Blockly Games

Day 1 - What you will learn today

- *What are Blockly Games?*
- *How to get the application?*
- *How to start using it?*

Blockly Games is a free application created by Google. It contains several educational games for teaching the principles of coding. No prior programming experience is expected.

Google observe Blockly Games 'encourages the development of tomorrow's professionals.' It can be used online or downloaded to your computer. You can play using your mobile phone or tablet also.

(1) Online use – You can use your PC or Mobile or Tablet. An Internet connection is required for playing the games. To start using Blockly games online, go to: https://blockly.games/

(2) Offline use –. An Internet connection is required only to get the installation files. No Internet is required after that. The zipped installation package is available at: https://github.com/google/blockly-games/wiki/Offline

You need to unzip the file in a folder and click on the HTML file available there. It uses Lego-like blocks to build commands for a computer to perform tasks to complete games. You can also change the language of Blockly Games by clicking the language option at the top right of the opening screen.

You will become familiar with key programming concepts like loops, conditions, decision making and computational thinking.

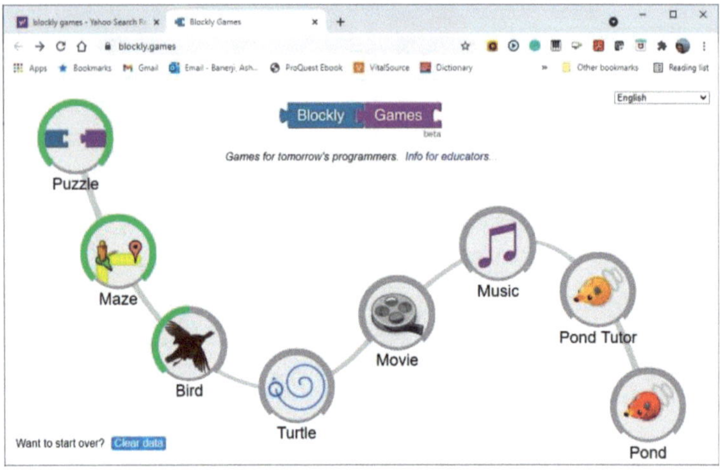

Fig. 1.1: The opening screen of Blockly Games

To start Blockly Games

- go to the website https://blockly.games/ or
- click on Blockly Games installed on your computer.

Fig 1.1 shows Eight game blocks. Within each block, there are several tasks and challenges to complete. As you progress, the outline of the game block will become green.

Are you not excited to start exploring your brain power?

Assignments

1. *Visit the Blockly Games online and have a practice.*
2. *Alternatively, get the Blockly Games zip package and install it on your computer.*

2. What is Computational Thinking

Day 2 - What you will learn today.

- *The essential literacies and their effect on our thinking.*
- *How are these enhanced by 21st-century literacy?*
- *How computational thinking supports 21st-century literacy?*

Let us have some fun experiments to understand what Computational Thinking is.

Reading and writing literacy

Years ago, you learned the alphabet and then started reading and writing. That was your first literacy achievement. Then you developed the capability to understand written words. As proof, read the following poem by Edward Lear (1812 – 1888).

> *There was an Old Man with a beard,*
> *Who said, "It is just as I feared!--*
> *Two Owls and a Hen,*
> *Four Larks and a Wren,*
> *Have all built their nests in my beard!*

Did you smile reading the poem? Think, why these words made you smile? Your smile proves that you have developed comprehension. You have gained the capability to think and imagine. This indeed is an achievement, but you need to move on.

Now, you write a 5-line poem yourself. This is called Cinquain, pronounced as 'sin-cane'. Rules for writing a Cinquain are:

- 1st line – to contain only one noun.
- 2nd line – two adjectives that describe the noun.
- 3rd line – three verbs or action
- 4th line - a longer description statement in four words
- 5th line – end with one word that means the same in line.

An example of Cinquain is:

Cave
Open, dark
Whispering, echoing, overwhelming
I search for reasons
Hollow.

Now, write a Cinquain yourself and tell your friends. This proves that you have the basic competency in the first two essential literacies which are reading and writing. CONGRATULATIONS!

It took continuous practice from your preschool years to achieve competency in two essential literacies.

Arithmetic literacy

The next is the numerical literacy (or aRithmatic literacy) that you all have learned.

I am sure, you know the numbers and you are comfortable with mathematical operations. As an experiment try the following Math Magic trick. This will prove your competency in numerical literacy. Please follow the instructions below.

Instructions for Math Magic

(a) Think of a number.
(b) Double it.
(c) Add 10.
(d) Halve it.
(e) Take away the original number.

I can predict the number you are left with. **It must be 5**. Right?

Try this again with other numbers. Doesn't it work always? Why?

The above experiments prove that you have the essential literacies - Reading, wRiting, and aRithmetics. This is called 3R literacy.

However, there are many more interesting things to learn. For this purpose, you need to learn through small steps and regularly.

Moving from 3R to 4R

Till the 20th century, the 3R literacies were adequate for us. However, the 21st century demanded another essential literacy, in addition to the 3Rs. This is called Digital literacy.

As a representative term for Digital literacy, 'computeR' literacy is added to the list making the 4R (Reading, wRiting, aRithmetic, and computeR) literacies for the 21st-century literacies.

The 3Rs enriched your comprehension and thinking abilities using language and Math. Similarly, computeR literacy empowers you to think computationally. I call this Computational Thinking (CT), an essential literacy for the 21st century in addition to the 3Rs.

The 3Rs enabled you to think and write poems or solve math. Similarly, the 4th R will enable you to think algorithmically. An algorithm is a step-by-step set of instructions for completing a task by a computer. It helps in communicating with computers.

CT is an internal process that includes Thinking Creatively, Reasoning Logically, Recognising Patterns, and Solving Problems. Regardless of age and interest, anyone will benefit from CT.

You will be able to create, innovate, automate and perform competently any activity by nurturing CT skills. It will develop your skills to think outside the box and conceptualize new ideas. These will also help you to develop practical and essential skills such as:

- Creative problem-solving ability
- Persistence, and deep thinking
- Logical perception and creativity
- Information analysis, resource recognition, and
- most importantly, learn how to learn.

The 3R literacies and technology advancements till the 20th century served as Power amplifiers for us. They enhanced our physical work capabilities. For example, the distances we can travel are aided by cars, aeroplanes, rockets and so on.

The fourth R serves as Brain's amplifier for us to enhance our brain's capabilities and intelligence. You can identify plenty of examples in all spheres of activities where digital technologies serve as amplifiers for brains' capabilities.

Examples are information storage, calculations, communication, efficient operations of machines, self-driving cars, robots, drones, artificial intelligence applications in various applications and so on. These are the result of 4R literacy.

Computational Thinking is the foundation skill for modern times. Are you not interested to learn and develop computational thinking skills? The games and puzzles described in this book will help you to get started.

Assignments

1. *Create two 'Cinquains' yourself.*
2. *Make another 'Math Magic' trick with different operations.*
3. *Think, what you gain by Computational Thinking capability.*

3. Blockly Games Puzzle

Day 3 - What you will learn today:

- *Learn how to use code blocks in Blockly.*
- *Experience how the Blockly pieces snap together.*
- *Practice how to assemble and disassemble Blocks.*

In the Puzzle game, you will learn the concept of 'block connection.' It will introduce the idea of snapping together Blockly's interlocking pieces or blocks, which are similar to LEGO blocks that you know.

Once you click on the Puzzle icon, you will see a page where you will find four images, four green blocks and several properties or traits (Fig. 3.1).

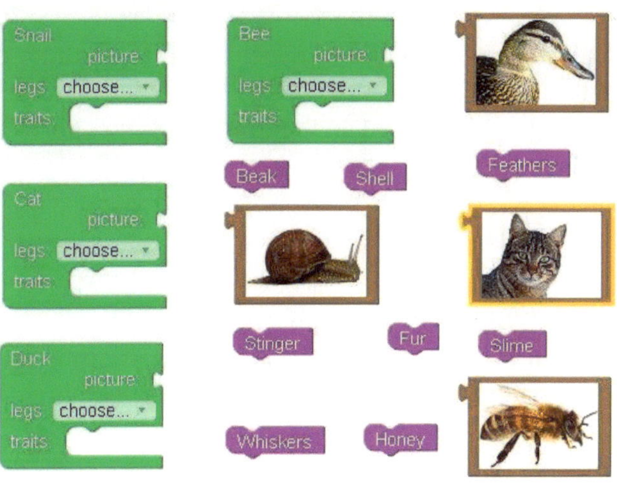

Fig. 3.1: Puzzle unsolved

Tasks

For this game level, you are required to connect Blocks to each class of animal to its image, specific characteristics such as 'far', 'beak etc. the number of legs for each.

Once completed, you will check for correctness. The solution to this puzzle is given in Fig 3.2. However, look at it only after completing it yourself.

Steps:

(1) Start Blockly Games and Click on Puzzle
(2) Drag and drop each animal picture next to the notch in the green block.
(3) Choose the number of legs for each class of animals by clicking on the little triangle.
(4) Then drag and drop the appropriate characteristics of four classes of animals in the empty slot in the green block.
(5) After placing and connecting all the blocks, click on "**Check Answers**" to find if you have done correctly.
(6) In case of any errors, you can correct them by disassembling and reassembling.
(7) To correct errors, separate the blocks and reconnect them.
(8) To separate any stacked blocks, drag off the bottom one from the stack.
(9) Once you have practised connecting the blocks correctly move on to the next game.

What did you learn from this exercise?

This exercise is important for learning. What are these? Let me write it from my point of view. You may add if you discovered anything else. That will be excellent. Keep a note in your learning diary.

- How do you drag and drop blocks?
- What to do if you make a mistake?
- How to redo to rearrange the blocks?

- What are the key properties or characteristics of different things?
- How do blocks snap together with magnet-like properties?
- Anything else?

These are important things that you learned. This will help you to complete the remaining part of the Blockly games. This learning will also help you work with Scratch. Scratch is a very interesting application that you can use for developing your own games, stories, and others. You will learn Scratch in another book.

Have you got everything right? If not try again. If yes, CONGRATULATIONS.

A correctly solved Puzzle will look like Fig. 3.2.

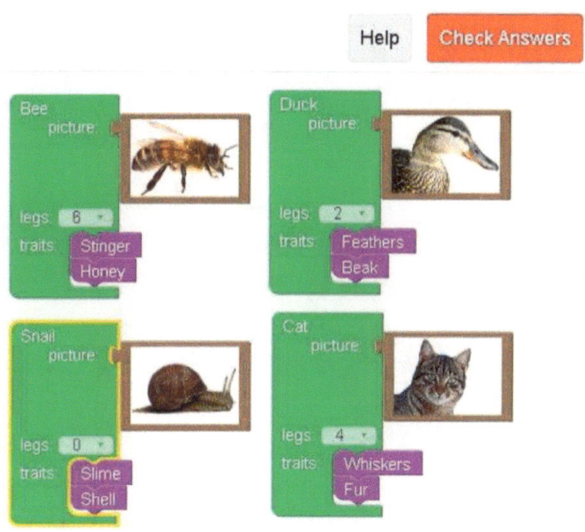

Fig. 3.2: Puzzle solved.

I made several mistakes when I tried the puzzle game first! Finally, I could place the blocks correctly. Phew!!! How about you?

Concept of Object-Oriented Programming

When you learn further and start with programming languages, you will discover that you have learned a very modern approach to programming through this exercise. This is called Object-Oriented Programming.

In this exercise, the green blocks are the object definition block. Many different classes of objects can be defined by this block by specifying different properties and characteristics for each class. For example, the Cat class or Duck class etc.

Object-oriented programming has been found very useful in professional programming development work.

It is an advanced concept, which I learned during my studies at university. However, you are learning about it even at school level. Fantastic!!!

Assignments

1. *Complete the Puzzle and check if you have done it properly.*
2. *Practice connecting and disconnecting blocks.*
3. *Practice how to change properties using the little triangle in the green block.*

"Arise, awake for the time is propitious. Already everything is opening out before us. Be bold and fear not."

Sw. Vivekananda

4. Maze Basics

Day 4 - What you will learn today:

- *Using the Blockly Games interface*
- *Using sequences, loops and conditions*
- *Constructing code of instructions and test them.*

In the Maze set of problems in Blockly Games, you are to instruct the *little man* or *Robot* to reach the goal through different mazes. For example, see Fig. 4.1.

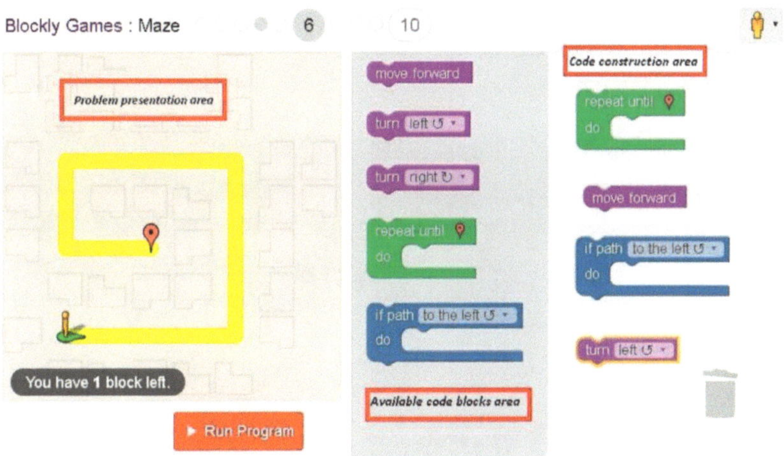

Fig 4.1: Blockly Interface showing (a) problem area, (b) area for available blocks and (c) code construction area.

The Blockly Game interface has three areas. (a) On the left is the problem presentation area. (b) In the middle is the available code blocks area. Please see the available coded blocks in Fig. 4.1. (c) On the rights is the code construction area.

The maze section of Blockly Games has ten levels of increasing difficulty.

You will use three types of blocks for instructing the robot.

- **ACTION** - Purple Blocks - Instructs what to do such as moving, turning left or right.
- **ITERATION** - Green Blocks - Loops which tell to keep on doing some action until some condition.
- **DECISION** - Blue Blocks - To check if something is true, deciding whether to take an action.

These code blocks allow the implementation of three types of instructions (Fig. 4.2):

(a) sequence,
(b) iteration and
(c) selection.

> "Man is not travelling from error to truth but from truth to truth from lower truth to higher truth."
>
> Sw. Vivekananda

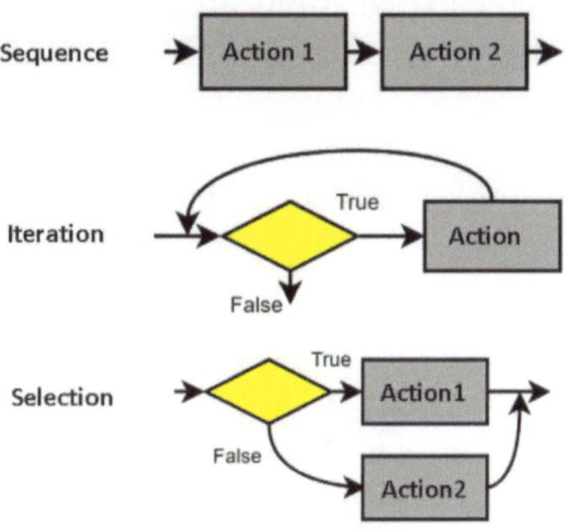

Fig 4.2: Three types of instructions

You will see what magic can be done with just these three types of instruction in Blockly Games.

Your Tasks for the maze games

From Maze Level 1 to 10 will require you to follow the steps mentioned below:

(1) Drag the instruction blocks in the code construction area as shown in Fig. 4.1 and then snap them together to create the program code for solving the particular maze.
(2) Practice using the blocks to complete a task in a certain way. This is called an algorithm that will guide a robot through a maze to reach a goal.
(3) Finally, you will check if your program works correctly as desired. In case of an error, dismantle the code blocks and reconnect. To dismantle, drag the blocks and drop them in the dustbin. You can also drag the blocks and drop them in the area of available blocks.
(4) Run the program and watch how the code blocks are getting active one by one. This is very helpful to appreciate the working of code blocks.

Along with reading the explanations given here, you can watch a short video of solutions for all levels of Maze at: https://youtu.be/O_KUaS9ZWGw

This will give you an idea of how the codes are being played to complete the problems.

Fig 4.3: Scan to watch a video of Maze solutions
Visit: https://youtu.be/O_KUaS9ZWGw

Note:

If your program works properly, a JavaScript version of the command is displayed. First-time learners may just watch the game's JavaScript version of the code.

Advanced users may come back later and note the JavaScript. This would be another topic that you can learn on your own. JavaScript will be discussed in another book.

Assignments

1. *Access Blockly Games Maze problems.*
2. *Get familiar with the Blockly Games interface.*
3. *Move on to solve the Level 1 Maze.*

5. Maze Level 1

Day 5 - What you will learn today:

- *Use of Purple Blocks for ACTION*
- *Make the robot reach the goal shown in Fig. 5.1.*
- *Use suitable code blocks to construct a program.*

Let's start with the first level of Maze problems.

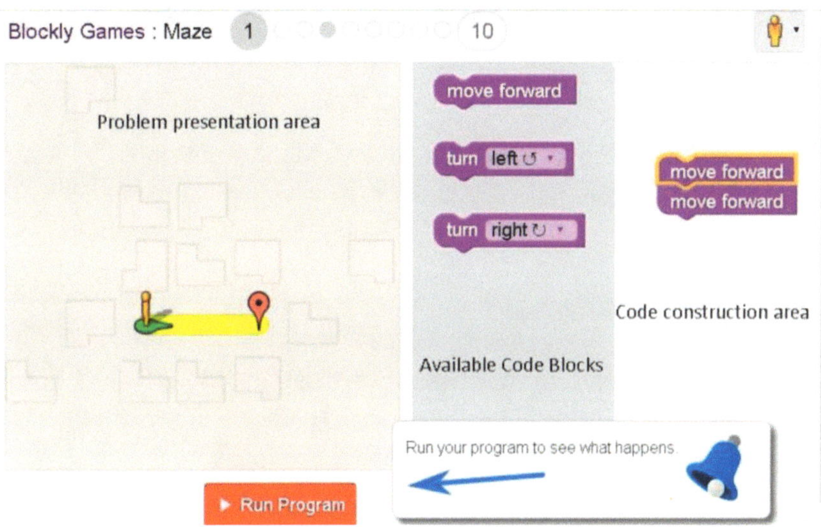

Fig 5.1: Level 1 Maze with code blocks and solution

Here, you need to make the robot move from the start position to the end position as shown in Fig. 5.1.

Tasks

(1) Drag the required code blocks to the code construction area.
(2) Test your program by pressing the Run Program button.
(3) A JavaScript version of the code will appear on success.
(4) Continue to the next level.

The Blockly program will consist of just two 'move forward' blocks placed in sequence as shown in Fig. 5.1.

The sequence of commands for completing the Robot's journey is shown as a diagram in Fig. 5.1. Such a diagram is called a 'flowchart'. For the Level 1 Maze, the flowchart of tasks will be simple as in Fig 5.2.

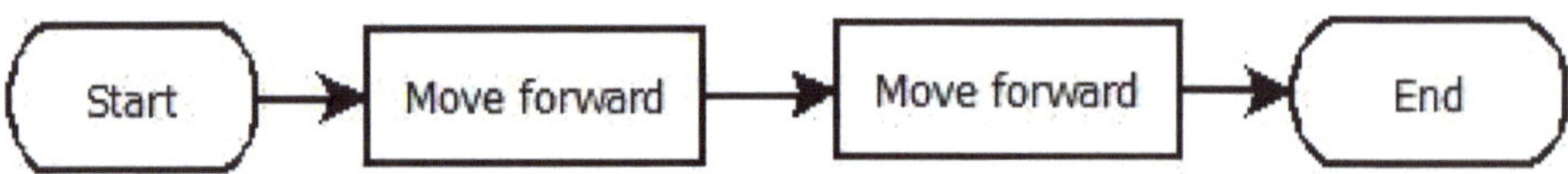

Fig 5.2: Flowchart for level 1 Maze solution

Learning

In this section, you learned:

1. How to construct the code of instructions to perform a task and
2. How to test the code.

This simple exercise is an example of Sequence of instructions.

Assignments

1. *Complete the Maze Level 1 problem.*
2. *Which types of blocks are available for the Level 1 maze?*
3. *Think why used only the Move forward blocks?*

6. Maze Level 2

Day 6 - What you will learn today:

- *Use of Purple Blocks for ACTION*
- *Make the robot reach the goal shown in Fig. 6.1*
- *Use Move Forward and Turn blocks to construct a program.*

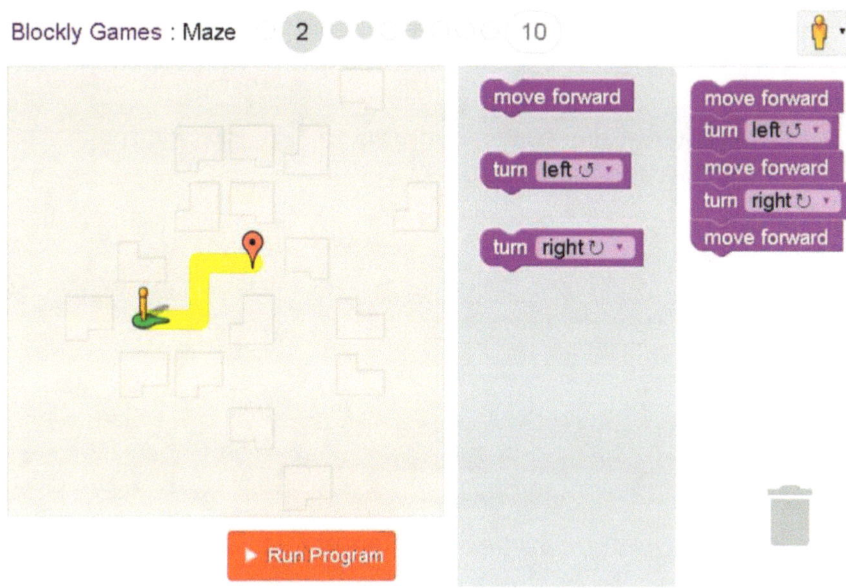

Fig. 6.1: Level 2 Maze with solution. Purple Blocks for ACTION

Life isn't always a straight path. To reach the goal for the Level 2 Maze, you need to move and change direction.

Please see the maze in problem presentation area (Fig. 6.1).

To reach the goal you need to use the 'Turn' blocks along with the Move blocks in proper sequence.

Tasks

(1) Drag the required code blocks to the code construction area.
(2) Test your program by pressing the Run Program button.
(3) Continue to the next level.

The Blockly program for this level will consist of the Move and Turn blocks as shown in Fig. 6.1.

Drawing a flowchart helps to understand how the commands work and how to organise the code blocks in sequence for a required task.

The flowchart for sequence of instructions to travel through the Level 2 Maze is shown in Fig 6.2.

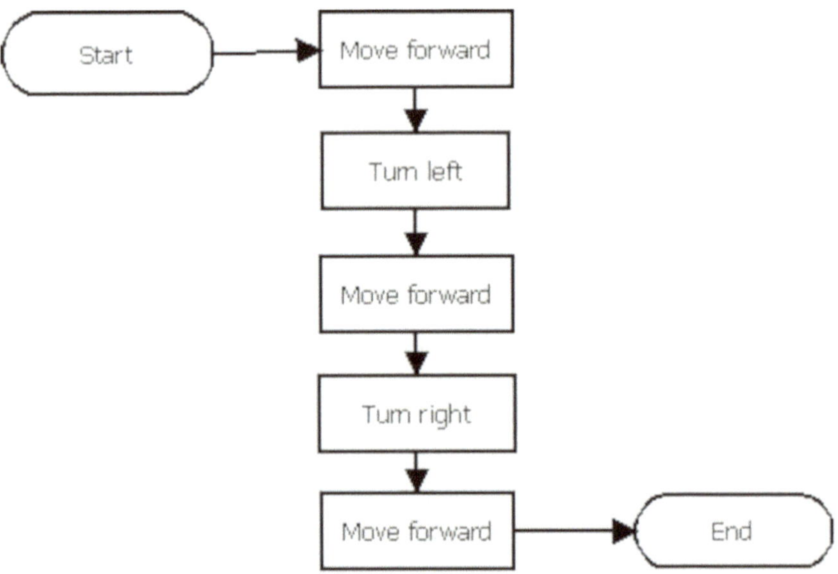

Fig. 6.2: Flowchart for Level 2 Maze

Learning

In the Maze Level 2 game, you learned:

(1) How to construct a sequence of instructions to travel through the maze.
(2) How to test the code.

This simple exercise will serve as a guide to navigating other maze problems. Let us move on to the next level of the complex maze.

First-time learners may just watch the JavaScript version of the code for the game.

Assignments

1. *Complete the Maze Level 2 problem.*
2. *Which types of blocks are available for the Level 2 maze?*
3. *Why you used the blocks in a certain sequence? Will it work if you change the sequence?*

> "Education is the manifestation of the perfection already in man."
>
> Sw. Vivekananda

7. Maze Level 3

Day 7 - What you will learn today:

- *Use of ACTION and ITERATION code blocks.*
- *Use Maximum 2 code blocks to construct a program.*
- *Make the robot reach the goal shown in Fig. 7.1.*

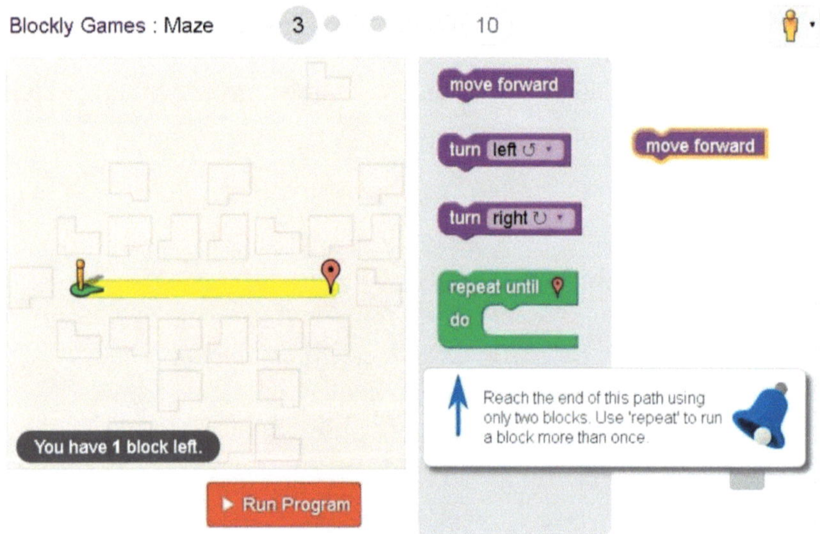

Fig. 7.1: Level 3 Maze
Purple Blocks for ACTION and Green Block ITERATION

Task

In the Level 3 Maze problem, you need to make Robot move continuously till it reaches the goal. How will you do that?

Recall the game Level 1 that you solved earlier where you placed two 'move forward' code blocks in sequence. In Level 3, the path to travel is about double of Level 1. Therefore, four 'move forward' blocks should do the job! Could you do that?

Certainly, it was not possible. You can see the problem. This level 3 Maze allows you to use only two code blocks. So, what will you do?

The trick can be done with the newly introduced Green code (repeat until block). Do the following:

(1) Drag the 'repeat until' code block to the construction area.
(2) Put the 'move forward' block inside the repeat until block.
(3) Run the program and watch how the Robot reaches the goal.

The code block will now look as shown in Fig. 7.2.

Fig. 7.2: Level 3 Maze solution with just two code blocks

Learning

The 'repeat until' is used to repeat a command until the goal is reached. In this case, the command is 'move forward'. Thus the Robot will move forward until it reaches the goal. This is called **Loop** in computer coding language.

In this game, you learned about 'iteration' using the 'repeat-until' block to create a **loop.** A flowchart for such a program is shown in Fig. 7.2.

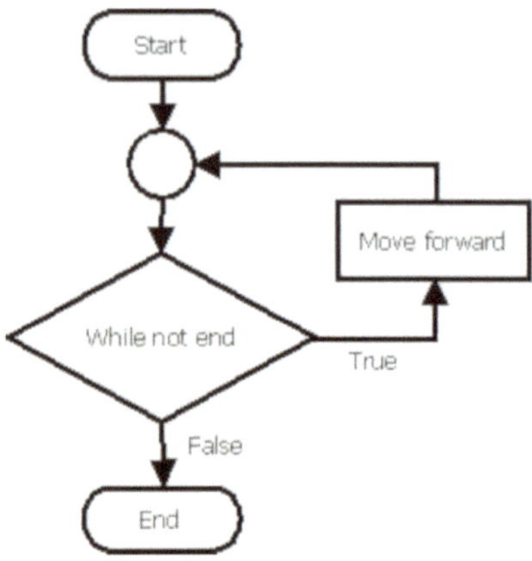

Fig. 7.2: Flowchart for Maze level 3 commands

A loop command tells the computer to run the same instructions multiple times. For this purpose, you don't have to write the same commands over and over. Thus, only one 'move forward' within the 'repeat until' is sufficient to move the robot from start to end.

Note

Computers ultimately just do a few very simple operations. The power of computers comes from the ability to repeat the same operation any number of times and do so very quickly. Programmers use **loops** to tell a computer to repeat an operation till a goal is accomplished.

You can put any instruction blocks inside the loop. These will be executed on each run (or iteration) through the loop. The loop is set to stop once the goal is reached.

Assignments

1. *Which types of blocks are available for the Level 3 maze?*
2. *Complete the Maze Level 3 problem.*
3. *Watch what happens in case the code sequence is wrong.*

8. Maze Level 4

Day 8 - What you will learn today:

- *Use of ACTION and ITERATION code blocks*
- *Use Maximum 5 code blocks to construct a program*
- *Make the robot reach the goal shown in Fig. 8.1*

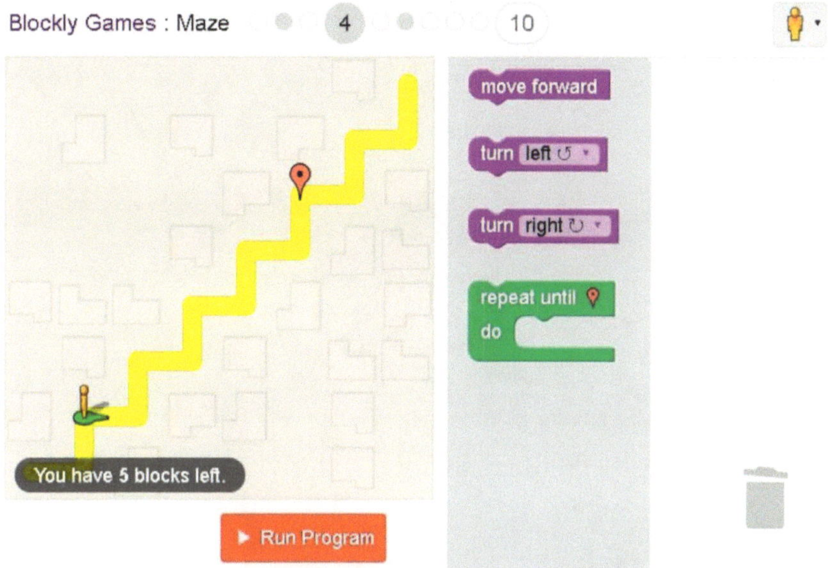

Fig. 8.1: Maze Level 4.
Use of Purple Blocks and Green Block

Task Solving level 4

For this game level, you need to make Robot move continuously till it reaches the goal. However, the path is zigzag. How will you do that?

The instruction would be 'move forward' then 'turn left' and then 'move forward' then 'turn right' and repeat these four steps again till the goal is reached.

Recall the Maze Level 2 where you used "move forward" and then 'turn left' code blocks to reach the goal. Also, recall Maze Level 3 where you used the 'move forward' code block within a repeat block. In both cases, the 'repeat until' block did the trick.

Level 3 was an improvement of the Level 1 solution. Similarly, Level 4 would be an improvement of the Level 2 solution. Now, try if you can make the Robot move the Level 4 Maze. Could you do that?

The solution code block will look as shown in Fig. 8.2.

Fig. 8.2: Level 4 Maze solution with five code blocks

The trick can be done with the newly introduced Green code block (repeat until block). Do the following:

(1) Drag the 'repeat until' code block to the construction area.
(2) Drag the 'move forward' block inside the 'repeat until' block.
(3) Drag the 'turn left' block inside the 'repeat until' block after the 'move forward' block.
(4) Drag the 'move forward' block the 'turn left' block inside the 'repeat until' block.
(5) Drag the 'turn right' block after the 'move forward' block inside the 'repeat until' block.
(6) Run the program and watch how the Robot reaches the goal.

Learning

The 'repeat until' is used to repeat a command or sequence of commands until the goal. In this case, four sets of commands consisting of 'move forward' - 'turn left' - 'move forward' - 'turn right' makes the Robot move and turn until it reaches the goal. This is called **Loop** in computer coding language.

The 'repeat-until' block is used to create a **loop** or **iteration.** A flowchart for such a program is in Fig. 8.3.

The use of 'repeat until' in Maze Level 4 is similar to that you have seen in Maze Level 3. Can you spot the difference?

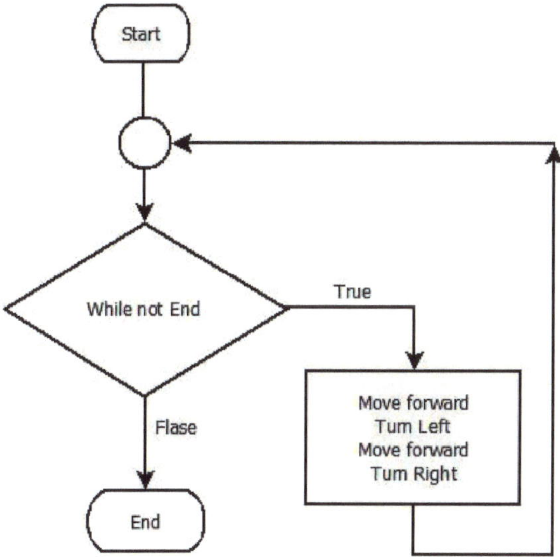

Fig. 8.3: Flowchart for level 4 commands

Note

The power of computers comes from their ability to repeat the same operation any number of times and do so very quickly.

Programmers use **loops** to tell a computer to repeat an operation till a goal is accomplished. Loop or Iteration is a very useful coding practice with which you can make the computer perform amazing tasks.

You can put any instruction blocks inside the loop. These will be executed on each run (or iteration) through the loop. The loop is set to stop once the goal is reached.

Assignments

1. *Which types of blocks are available for the Level 4 maze?*
2. *Complete the Maze Level 4 problem.*
3. *Watch what happens in case the code sequence is wrong.*

"The powers of the mind are like rays of light dissipated; when they are concentrated, they illumine. This is our only means of knowledge."

Sw. Vivekananda

9. Maze Level 5

Day 9 - What you will learn today:

- *Use of ACTION and ITERATION code blocks*
- *Use Maximum 5 code blocks to construct a program*
- *Make the robot reach the goal shown in Fig. 9.1*

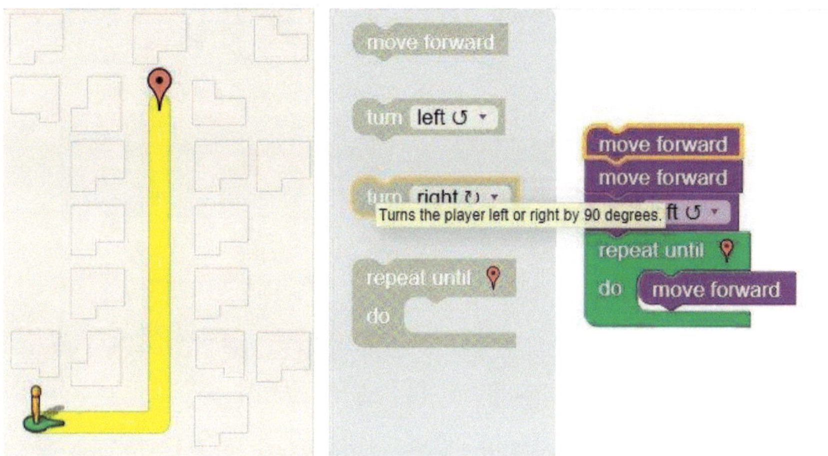

Fig. 9.1: Maze Level 5 with solution

Task Solving level 5

For the Maze level 5, you need to make Robot move continuously till it reaches the goal. The path is partly horizontal and then vertical (Fig,9.1). You can use a maximum of 5 code blocks. How will you do that?

The task for the robot to reach the goal would be:

(a) move forward
(b) then turn left and
(c) again move forward.

Similar to Maze Level 1 you can

- travel the horizontal path with two 'move forward' blocks.
- then turn left
- after that move continuously using 'repeat until' block.

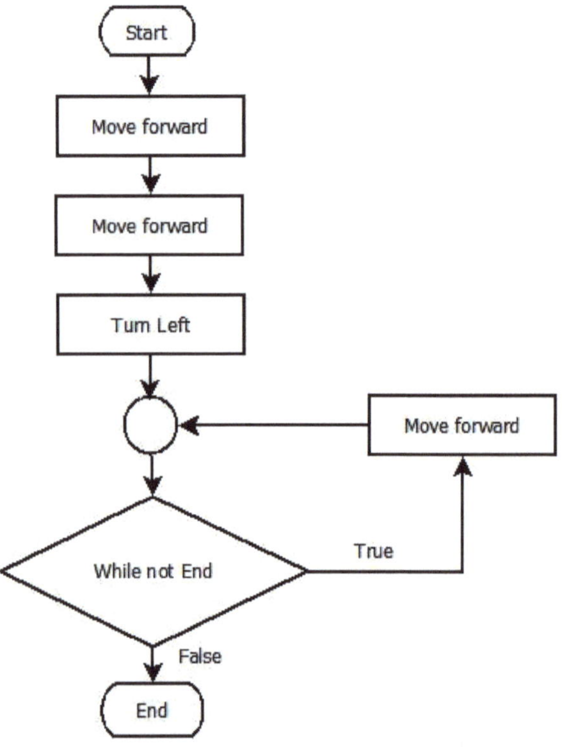

Fig. 9.2: Flowchart for level 5 commands

The solution to the Maze level 5 is shown in the code construction area in Fig. 9.1. Fig. 9.2 shows the flowchart for the program.

Note

The power of computers comes from their ability to repeat the same operation any number of times and do so very quickly. Programmers use **loops** to tell a computer to repeat an operation till a goal is accomplished. Loop or iteration is useful coding practice with which you can make the computer perform amazing tasks.

You can put any instruction blocks inside a loop. These will be executed on each run (or iteration) through the loop. The loop is set to stop once the goal is reached.

Assignments

1. *Which types of blocks are available for the Level 5 maze?*
2. *Complete the Maze Level 5 problem.*
3. *Watch what happens in case the code sequence is wrong.*

"Each is great in his own place, but the duty of one is not the duty of others."

Sw. Vivekananda

10 Maze Level 6

Day 10 - What you will learn today:

- *Use of ACTION, ITERATION and DECISION code blocks.*
- *Use Maximum 5 code blocks to construct a program.*
- *Make the robot reach the goal shown in Fig. 10.*

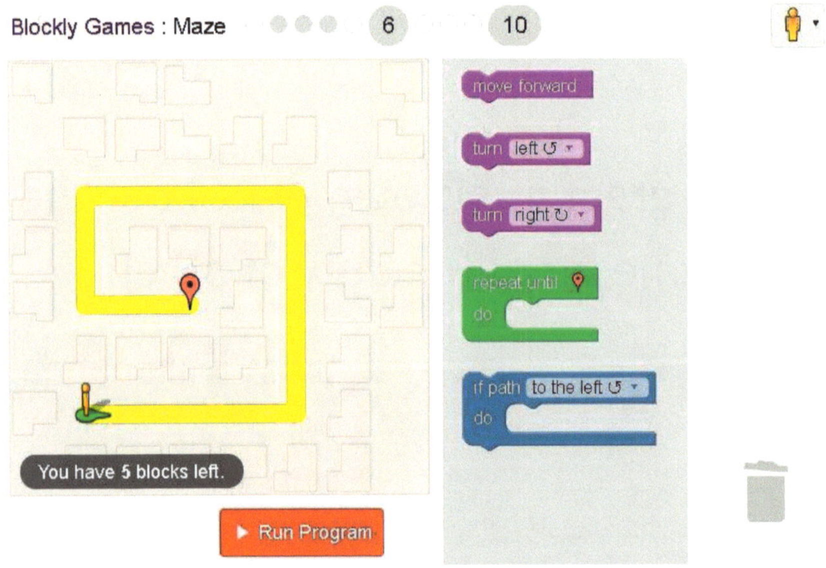

Fig. 10.1: Maze Level 6 problem and available code blocks

For level 6, you need to make Robot move forward, turn left and again move forward till it reaches the goal (Fig,10.1). You can use a maximum of 5 code blocks. How will you do that?

Task Solving level 6

The Maze Level 6 introduces a new type of code block for DECISION. The Blue code block checks **IF** some condition is true then **DO** some action. The if-block in this game lets you check if there is a path in a certain direction. This block is used to turn when needed!

For the Level 6 problem drag the code blocks into the code construction area and arrange them as shown in Fig. 10.2 (a).

Commands that the codes will execute are shown in a structured language as shown in Fig. 10.2 (b).

Writing commands in this way is called pseudocode. This is an alternative method of using the 'flowchart' diagram that you have seen in earlier problems.

Powerful programs can be constructed by combining **Iteration** with **Sequence** and **Decision** blocks. Example, see the solution to the Level 6 Maze in Fig. 10.2 (a).

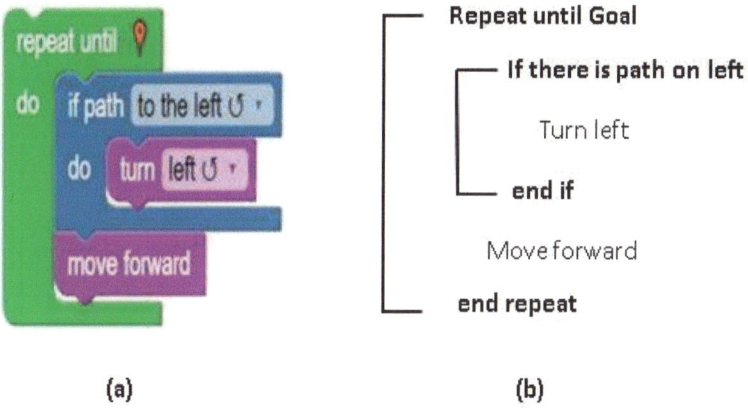

Fig. 10.2 Maze Level 6 solution with pseudocode

Note

Until now you have used **Sequence** and **Iteration** types of instructions that get executed no matter what.

However, sometimes you need to tell the computer to take a decision. You may want it to do something when a certain condition is true.

Computers can repeat the same operation any number of times using **iteration** or **loops**. Combined with **decision** commands using IF condition checking, more sophisticated programs can be developed.

In this maze problem, you used three types of code blocks: **action**, **repeat-until** and **IF condition** checking for a task till a goal is accomplished. This is a very useful coding practice with which you can make the computer perform amazing tasks.

Pseudocode shows the commands in simple language that you can understand, Fig. 10.2 (b)

Run the program and watch how the robot moves with the use of IF condition check.

Assignments

1. *Which types of blocks are available for the Level 6 maze?*
2. *Complete the Maze Level 6. Can you make it differently by placing the 'move forward' block towards the beginning?*
3. *Watch what happens in case the code sequence is wrong.*

11. Maze Level 7

Day 11 - What you will learn today:

- *Use of ACTION, ITERATION and DECISION code blocks*
- *Use Maximum 5 code blocks to construct a program*
- *Make the robot reach the goal shown in Fig. 11.1*

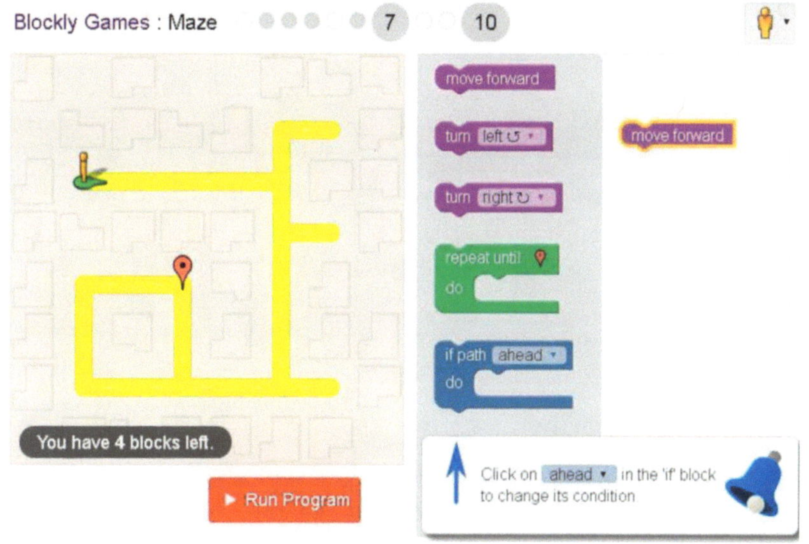

Fig. 11.1: Level 7 Maze problem

For level 7, you need to make Robot move forward, turn right and again move forward till it reaches the goal (Fig,11.1). You can you do the task using a maximum of 5 code blocks?

How to do that?

Hint: this maze is like Maze Level 6. Try to assemble the code blocks without looking at the solution.

Task Solving level 7

Instruct the robot to travel through the maze to reach the goal (Fig. 11.1). For this purpose, you have three types of Block commands – (i) Purple blocks (Motion), (ii) a Green block (Loop) and (iv) a Blue block (Condition checking).

The condition checking "If" block takes the decision of whether to turn right or move forward.

The condition-checking block and movement are placed within a Repeat loop so that these actions continue till the goal is reached.

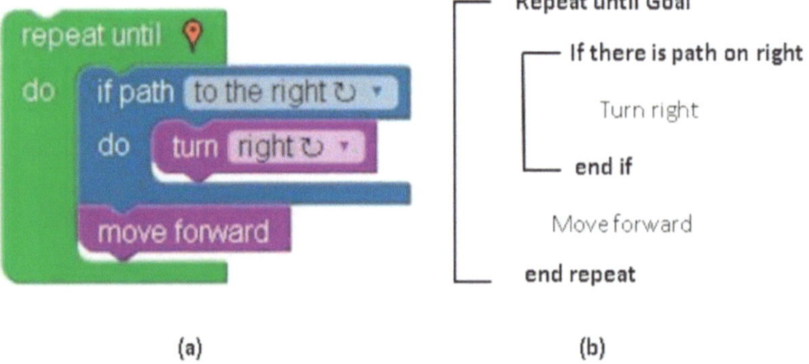

(a)   (b)

Fig. 11.2 Maze Level 7 solution with pseudocode

For the Level 7 problem, drag the code blocks into the code construction area and arrange them as shown in Fig. 11.2 (a).

Commands that the codes will execute are shown as pseudocode in Fig. 11.2 (b).

Pseudocode presents the commands in the form of a structured language that we can easily understand.

Note

The Level 7 maze is similar to Level 6. Can you spot the difference?

In this maze problem, you used three types of code blocks: **action**, **repeat-until** and **IF condition** checking for a task till a goal is accomplished. This is a very useful coding practice with which you can make the computer perform amazing tasks.

Pseudocode shows the commands in simple language that you can understand, Fig. 11.2 (b).

Run the program and watch how the robot moves by using condition checking.

Compare the condition-checking Blue blocks in Level 6 and Level 7. Aren't they different? You can change it by clicking on the little triangle. Then you can select any of the three types that you require (see Fig. 11.3).

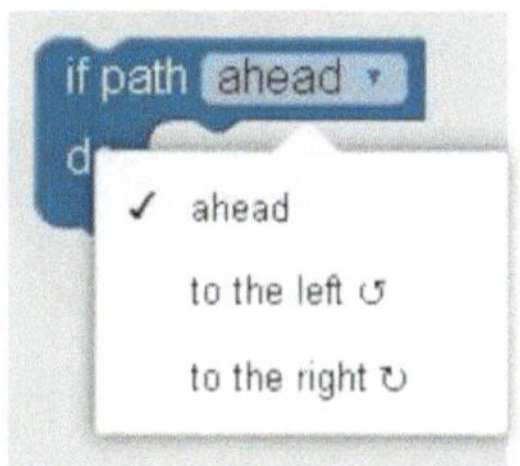

Fig. 11.3: Changing if condition checking

Assignments

1. *Which types of blocks are available for the Level 7 maze?*
2. *Complete the Maze Level 7. Can it be solved differently?*
3. *Watch how the robot moves with condition checking.*

12. Maze Level 8

Day 12 - What you will learn today:

- *Use of ACTION, ITERATION and DECISION code blocks.*
- *Use Maximum 10 code blocks to construct a program.*
- *Make the robot reach the goal shown in Fig. 12.1.*

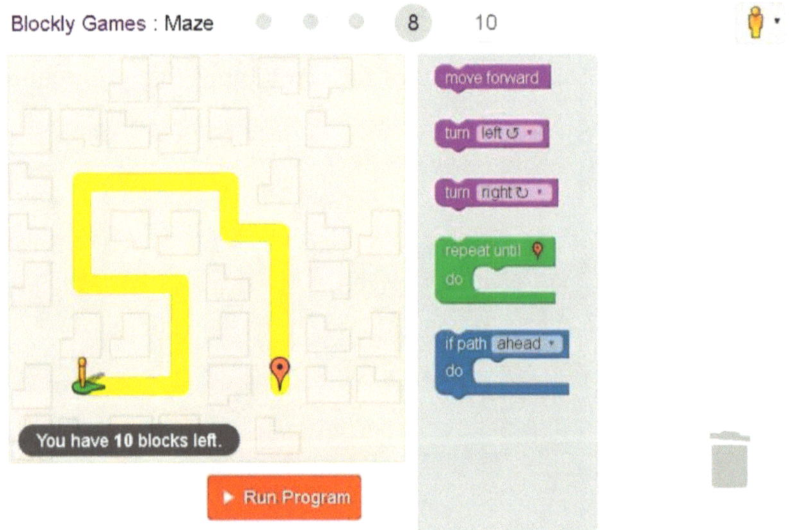

Fig. 12.1: Maze 8 problem

For the Level 8 maze, you need to make Robot move forward, turn left, then move forward and turn right, and likewise continue till it reaches the goal (Fig,11.1).

You can use a maximum of 10 code blocks consisting of ACTION, ITERATION and DECISION bocks. How will you do that?

Hint: this maze is a combination of Level 6 and Level 7. Try to assemble the code blocks without looking at the solution.

Task Solving level 7

Instruct the robot to travel through the maze to reach the goal (Fig. 11.1). For this purpose, you have three types of Block commands -

- Purple blocks (Motion),
- Green block (Loop) and
- Blue block (Condition checking).

The condition checking "If" block takes the decision of whether to turn right or turn left as it moves forward. For this purpose, two condition-checking blocks, and a move-forward block is placed within a Repeat loop so that these actions continue till the robot reaches the goal.

Fig. 12.2: Maze 8 solution

Note

The Level 8 maze is a combination of Level 6 and Level 7. Can you spot the difference?

In this maze problem, you used three types of code blocks: **action**, **repeat-until** and **IF condition** checking till a goal is accomplished. This is a very useful coding practice that you should note.

You can change the condition-checking of the Blue block by clicking on the little triangle. Then you can select any of the three types that you require (see Fig. 12.3).

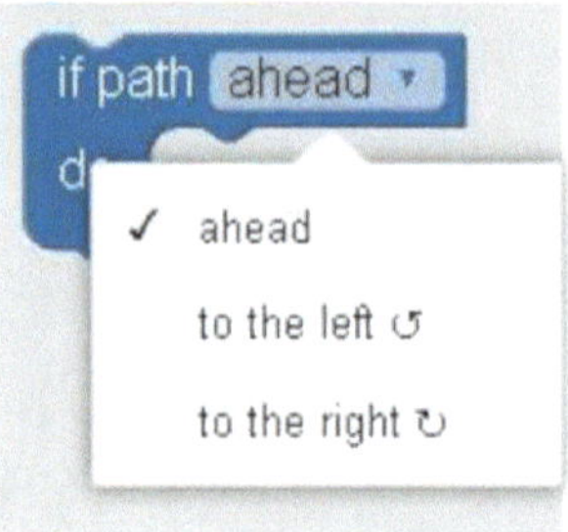

Fig. 12.3: Changing if condition checking.

Run the program and watch how the robot moves by using two conditions checking.

Assignments

1. *Which types of blocks are available for the Level 8 maze?*
2. *Complete the Maze Level 8. Can it be solved differently?*
3. *Watch how the robot moves with the condition checking.*

"Every man should take up his own ideal and endeavour to accomplish it."

Sw. Vivekananda

13. Maze Level 9

Day 13 - What you will learn today:

- *Use of ACTION, ITERATION and DECISION code blocks.*
- *Use Maximum 7 code blocks to construct a program.*
- *Make the robot reach the goal shown in Fig. 13.1.*

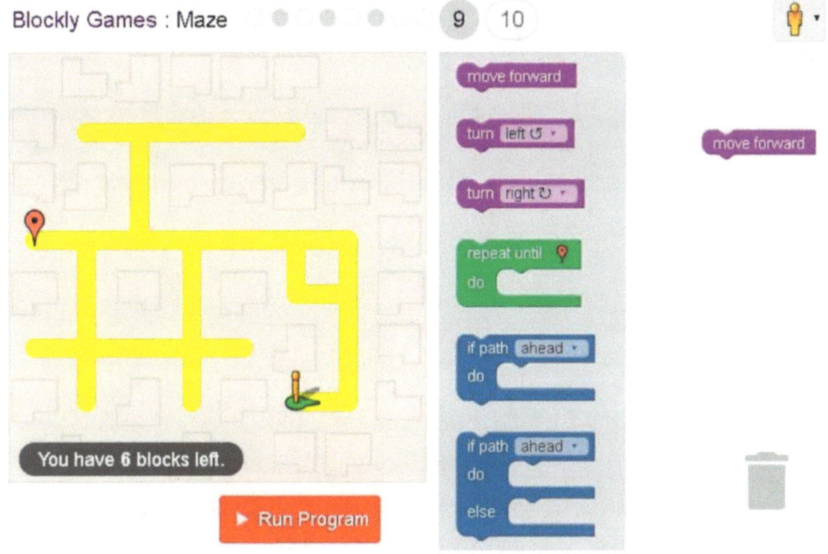

13.1 Maze 9 problem

For the Level 9 maze, you need to make Robot move forward, turn left then continue to move forward till it reaches the goal (Fig,13.1).

You can use a maximum of 7 code blocks consisting of ACTION, ITERATION and DECISION bocks.

How will you use it to solve the Maze level 9?

Task Solving level 9

Instruct the robot to travel through the maze to reach the goal (Fig. 13.1). Note, a new type of DECISION block can be used in this level for condition checking.

The IF-ELSE condition checking allows two types of decision-making. See Fig. 13.4.

The robot moves forward if there is a path ahead. Otherwise, it turns left. The whole process is repeated till the goal is reached.

Construct the commands to act in this way as shown in Fig. 13.2 (a).

Pseudocode for the instructions is shown in Fig. 13.2 (b).

Run the program and watch how the robot moves by using the if-else conditions checking.

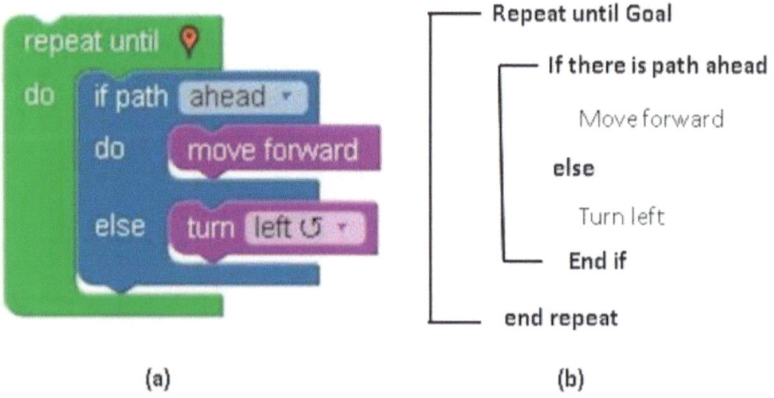

13.2: Maze Level 9 solution 1 with pseudocode

Note

The Maze Level 9 utilises a new type of decision block, the **if-else**.

The IF decision block that you used earlier, makes a one-way interaction as shown in Fig 13.3 flowchart.

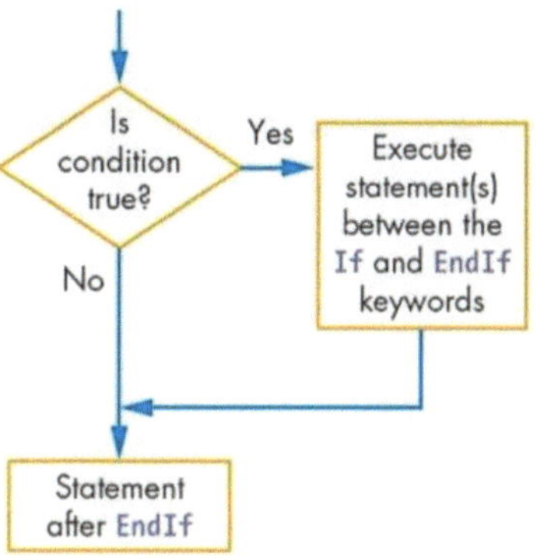

Fig. 13.3: The If flowchart example

The IF-ELSE decision block that you used, makes a two-way selection. This is shown in Fig 13.4.

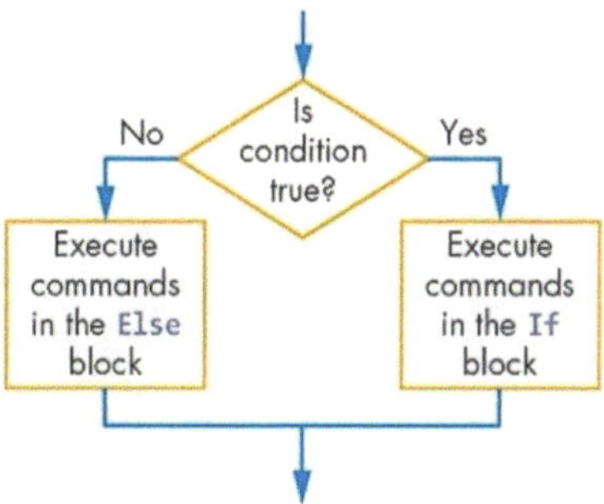

Fig. 13.4: The If-else flowchart example

In the maze Level 9 problem, you used three types of code blocks: **action**, **repeat-until** and **IF condition** checking till a goal is accomplished in Fig.13.3.

You can also combine the two types of condition-checking to solve the same Level 9 Maze. This is shown in Fig. 13.4.

Fig. 13.4: Maze Level 9 solution 2

Thus, you can see that the same problem can be solved in different ways. The solutions depend on your unique Computational Thinking skills. Computational Thinking enables you to solve problems differently. It develops out-of-the-box thinking skills.

Three ways to achieve it are practice-practice and practice! Are you ready?

Assignments

1. *Which code blocks you used for the Level 9 maze?*
2. *Complete the Maze Level 9 problem in different ways.*
3. *Watch how the robot moves with the conditions checking.*

"The goal may be distant, but awake, arise, and stop not till the goal is reached."

Sw. Vivekananda

14. Maze Level 10

Day 14 - What you will learn today:

- *Use of ACTION, ITERATION and DECISION code blocks.*
- *Use Maximum 10 code blocks to construct a program.*
- *Make the robot reach the goal shown in Fig. 14.1.*

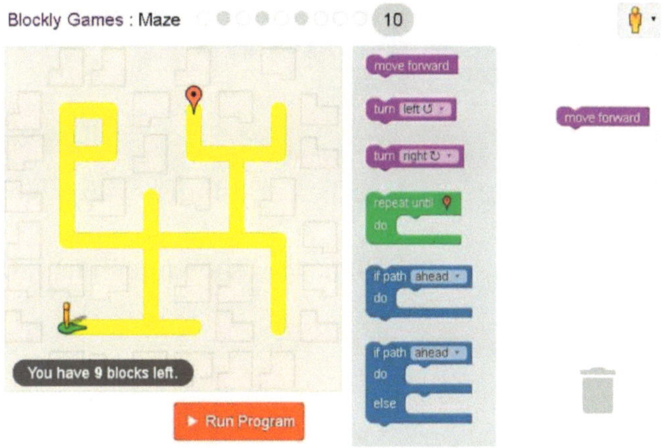

Fig. 14.1: Maze Level 10 problem

Task Solving level 10

The Maze Level 10 is hard. So, it is optional for you to try it if you love challenges. Otherwise, just implement the solution given in Fig. 14.2 and see how it works!

One approach for the Level 10 maze would be to continue checking and following the left-hand wall. This is done in Fig. 14.2.

Could you solve this complicated maze?

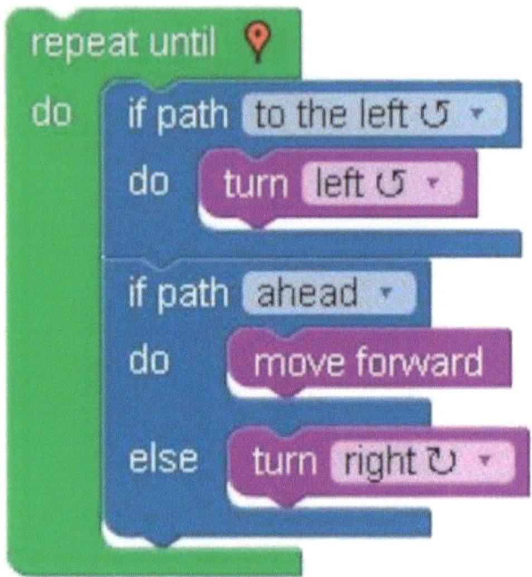

Fig. 14.2 Maze Level 10 inefficient solution with 6 blocks

JavaScript code for the Level 10 maze is shown in Fig.14.3.

```javascript
while (notDone()) {
  if (isPathLeft()) {
    turnLeft();
  }
  if (isPathForward()) {
    moveForward();
  } else {
    turnRight();
  }
}
```

Fig. 14.3: JavaScript code for the Level 10 maze

You may also try the alternative solution and see how it works. See Fig. 14.4.

```
repeat until  📍
do  move forward
    if path  ahead ▾
    do   if path  to the right ↻ ▾
         do    turn  right ↻ ▾
         else  if path  to the left ↺ ▾
               do    turn  left ↺ ▾
    else  if path  to the left ↺ ▾
          do    turn  left ↺ ▾
          else  turn  right ↻ ▾
```

14.4 Maze Level 10 efficient solution with 10 blocks

The code structures you used in previous maze levels, solved a specific maze. As you gain more experience, you can write generic programs that can search for a path in any Maze!

Assignments

1. *Which code blocks you used for the Level 10 maze?*
2. *Solve the Maze Level 10 problem in different ways.*
3. *Watch how the robot moves with the conditions checking*

Review of Maze Games

In the Maze games of Blockly, you were controlling a *Robot* to reach the goal through a maze. For this purpose, you used three types of code blocks as shown in Fig. 15.1.

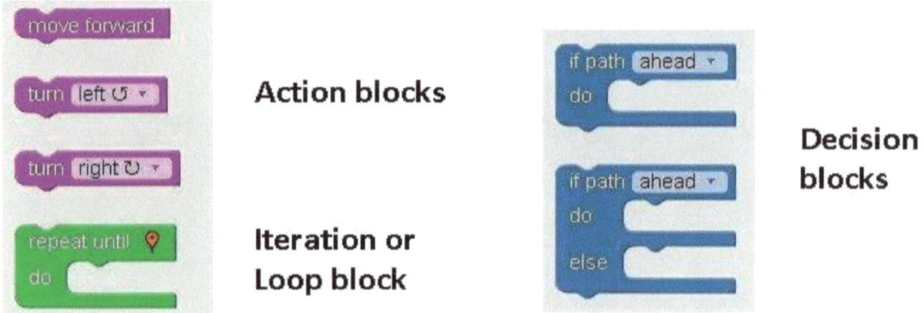

Fig.15.1: Three types of code blocks used in Maze games

You have become familiar with two types of condition checking Decision blocks in Maze games. You have also learned how to draw a flowchart and write a pseudocode. There three phases of learning:

Memorise (chapter 1 to 14): This completes the first phase of your journey with this book. Repeat the exercises of the guided lessons till you remember them by heart. Completing these lessons, you should have learned the essential coding concepts and steps.

Introspection (chapter 15 and 16). The second phase of journey is to absorb knowledge through practice and reflection. This is realised in Semi guided lessons with exercises.

Critical Thinking and Analysis (chapters 17 to 21): The third phase of journey involves deliberation and solving new problems. In this phase you are to think critically and make your own decision and conclusion. For this purpose, you may draw a flowchart of the program you develop. You may write pseudocode as well.

15. Blockly Games: Bird

Day 15 - What you will learn today:

- *Understand the basics of 'Bird' games.*
- *Practice using some new types of code blocks.*
- *Solve Bird Game Level 7 as a sampler of Bird.*

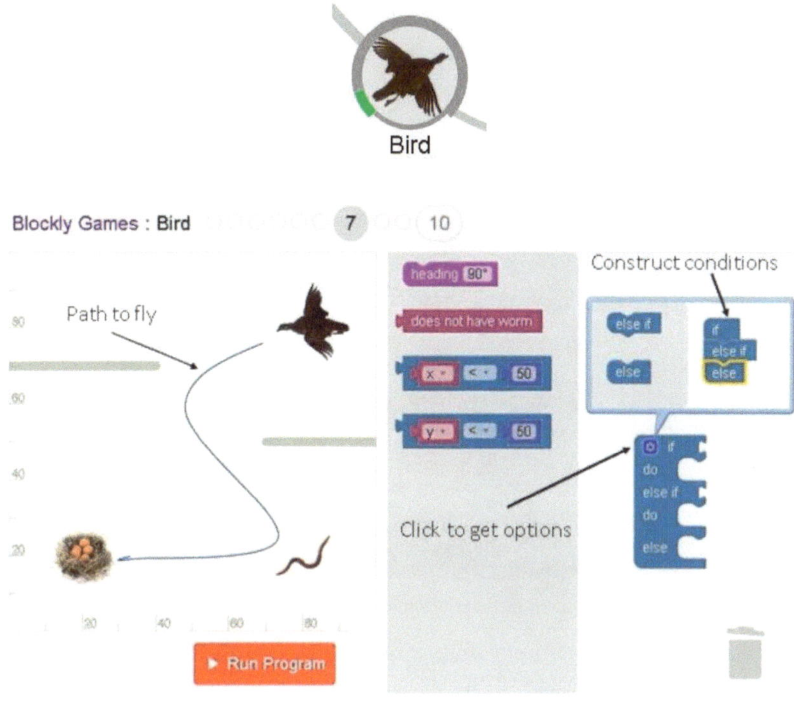

Fig. 15.2: Bird flight path and Condition building

Now in the "Bird" games, you will be controlling a *Drone* (say a 'Bird') to reach a goal. In this set of games, you will be making the Bird fly through obstacles to catch an insect and then return to the nest. For this purpose, you need more advanced condition-checking. Therefore, you will be creating your own condition-checking block in the Birds group of Games. An example of IF-ELSE-IF block is shown in (Fig. 15.2).

Tasks for Bird Level 7

(1) Click on the gear wheel on the if-do block.
(2) Available options for changing conditions will appear as in upper right in Fig. 15.2
(3) Construct your required conditions.
(4) Drag the required code blocks and construct the codes as shown in Fig. 15.3
(5) Make sure to change the angles and conditions as in Fig. 15.3
(6) Run the program.

Thus 'Bird' in Blockly Games will take you through a deep dive into conditionals. Control flow is explored with increasingly complex conditions.

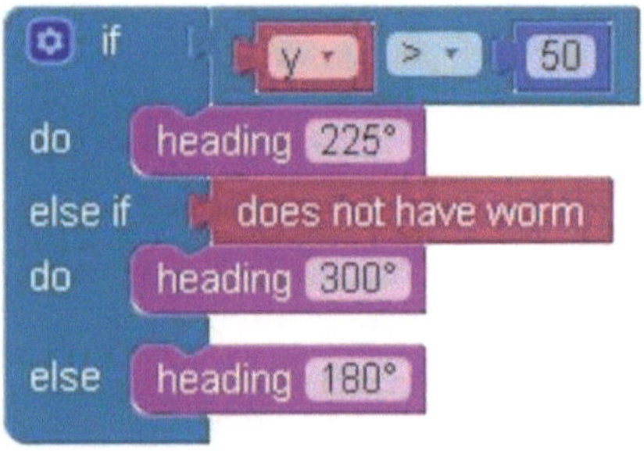

Fig. 15.3 Codes for Bird's flight path

In this game both **sequences of actions** and **decision-checking** are important. The 'Bird' game has ten levels. It starts with a simple game and then gradually more interesting coding will be covered.

Assignments

1. *Solve the 'Bird' game Level 7 as an example.*
2. *Practice constructing different IF conditions and dismantling them.*
3. *See the effect of X and Y parameters for the IF block.*

Bird Exercises

Solve the following exercises. Angles that the bird need to turn are shown for illustration. Solutions are given in Appendix 1 but please do not look at the solutions until you complete them.

Bird Level 2

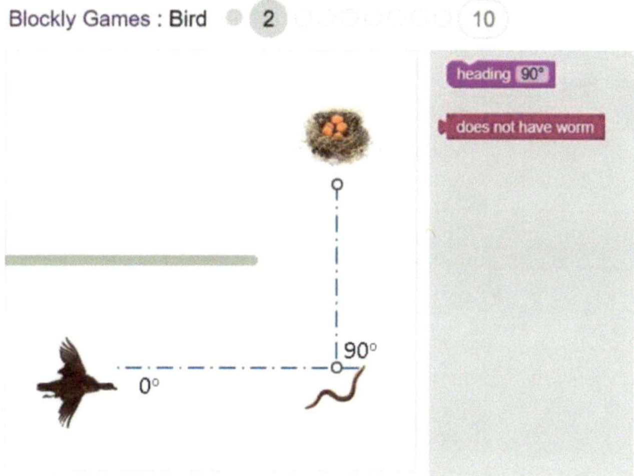

Bird Level 3

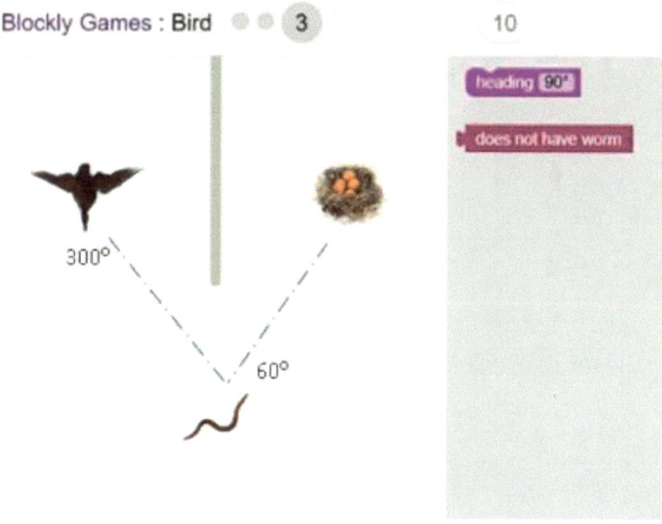

Bird Level 4

Bird Level 5

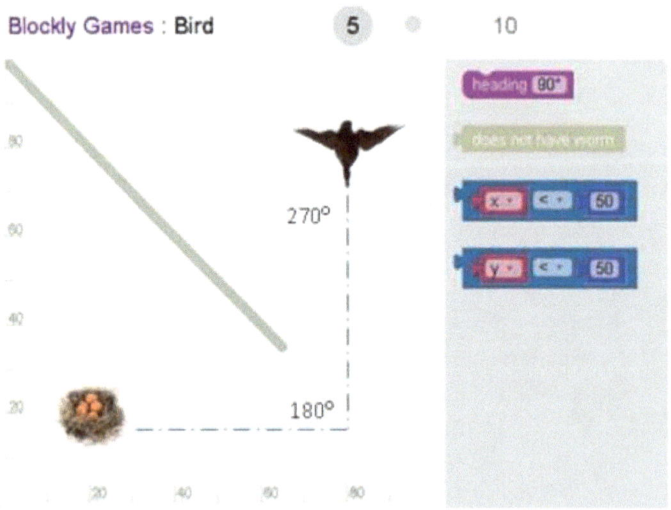

Solving these exercises will demonstrate how much you have learned.

16. Blockly Games: Turtle

Day 16 - What you will learn today:

- *Understand the basics of 'Turtle' games.*
- *Use new types of code blocks for Turtle movement in angle.*
- *Solve Turtle Game Level 1 as a sampler.*

Turtle

The Turtle Level of Blockly Games will allow you to explore more applications of loops. You can paint multiple shapes and pictures using nested loops.

Solutions for all the levels for Turtle will be provided in another book. However, it will be better for learning to practice all the previous games yourself without looking at the solutions.

Tasks for Turtle Level 1

Create a program to draw a square using the available code blocks - move, turn, repeat (Fig. 16.1).

(1) Drag the loop code block.
(2) Place the move code block within it
(3) Place the turn code block within it
(4) Run code at different speed.

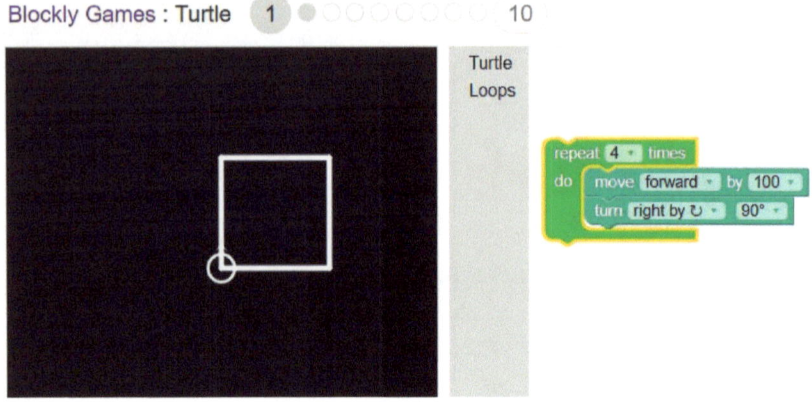

Fig. 16.1: Code for Turtle Games Level 1

Solution for the Turtle Level 1 is shown in Fig. 16.1.

The 'Turtle' game has ten levels. You will be creating interesting drawings and paintings.

Solutions for all the levels for Turtle will be provided in another book. It will be better for learning to practice all the previous games yourself without looking at the solutions.

The Repeat and Action codes can make the computer perform interesting tasks.

Similarly, you can also become an amazing learner in any subject with repeated learning actions. After all you are cleverer than the computer!!! Are you not?

Assignments

1. *Solve the 'Turtle' game Level 1 as an example*
2. *Experiment by changing the repeat number and move/turn angles*
3. *See the effect of changing the play speed of code blocks*

Turtle Exercises

Solve the following exercises. Solutions are given in Appendix 2. However, don't look at the solutions until you complete them.

Turtle Level 2

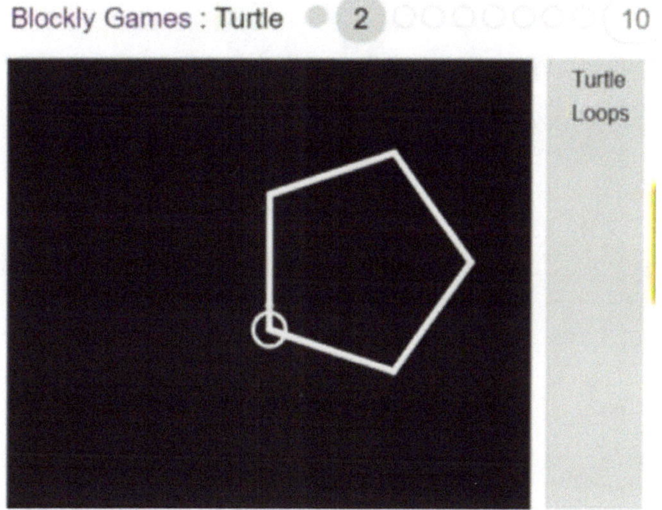

Turtle Level 3

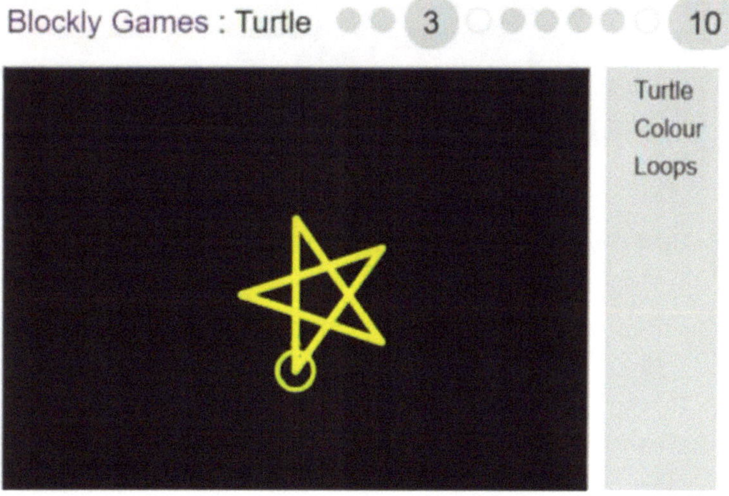

Turtle Level 4

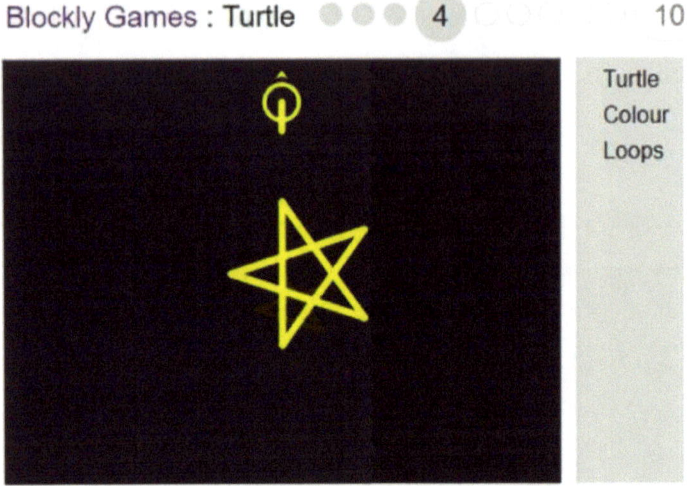

Turtle Level 5

Solving these exercises will demonstrate how much you have learned,

Introduction to Other Games

The following chapters will briefly introduce you to the other game blocks available in Blockly Games. These are:

1. Movie
2. Music
3. Pond Tutor and
4. Pond

These chapters are a sampler of the more advanced programming concepts that are introduced through these six game blocks. These will be covered in detail in another book.

> "The secret of life is not enjoyment but education through experience."
>
> Sw. Vivekananda

17. Blockly Games: Movie

What you will learn today:

- *Understand the basics of 'Movie' games.*
- *Use code blocks for drawing shapes at different positions.*
- *Solve Movie Game Level 1 as a sampler.*

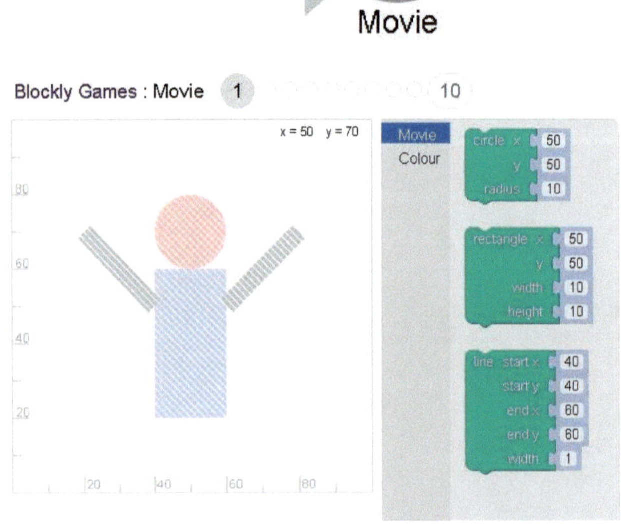

Fig 17.1: Available code blocks for Movie Level 1

In this game, you will use mathematical concepts. There are 10 levels of the Movie game. Complexity levels are increased at each level. Only the Level 1 Movie is shown here as an example. Solutions for all levels of Movies will be provided in another book.

Tasks for Movie Level 1

As you open this game you will see an outline of a shape. You need to use simple shapes to draw this person.

(1) Click on the color menus (Fig. 17.1) and drag the color block to the work area and set color.
(2) Click on the Movie menus and drag the shape blocks to the work area.
(3) Change the parameters so that the shapes are aligned (Fig.17,2).

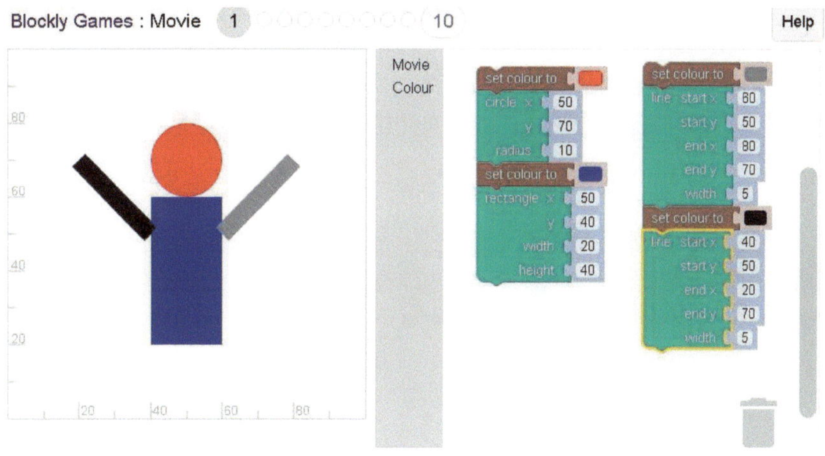

Fig. 17.2: Constructed codes and parameters for Movie Level 1

Assignments

1. *Solve the 'Movie' game Level 1 as an example.*
2. *Experiment with position parameters and shape sizes.*
3. *See the effect of changing the color of shapes.*

18. Blockly Games: Music

What you will learn today:

- *Understand the basics of 'Music' games.*
- *Use code blocks for different music compositions.*
- *Solve Music Game Level 1 as a sampler.*

The Blockly Games in Music group is an introduction to functions. You will use functions to compose music.

The green block is for note functions. You can change the parameter - C4, D4 and so on. The Music Game page looks as in Fig. 18.1.

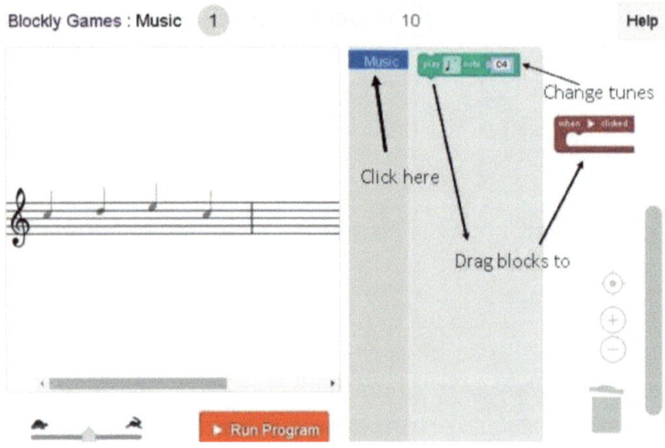

Fig. 18.1: Code for Music Level 1

Tasks for Level 1 Music

(1) Click on the Music tab.
(2) Drag the Green code blocks inside the 'when clicked' block.
(3) Change the function parameters - C4, D4 and so on as shown in Fig. 18.2.
(4) Run the program.

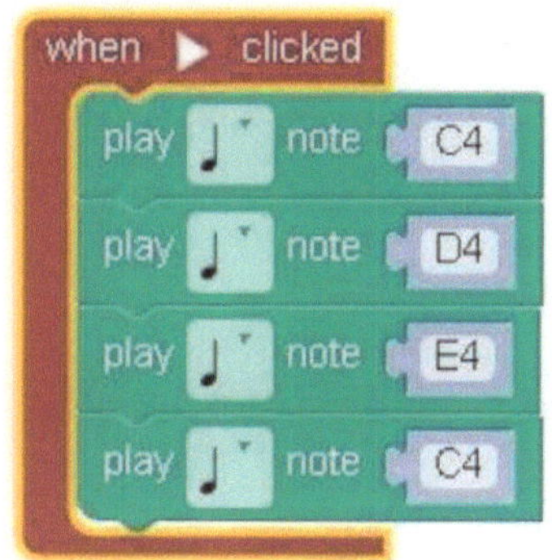

Fig. 18.2 Code blocks for Music Level 1

How wonderful. You can create your own music!!!

Assignments

1. *Solve the 'Music' game Level 1 as an example.*
2. *Experiment with notes and compositions.*
3. *See the effect of changing the color of shapes.*

"Strength is life, weakness is death."

Sw. Vivekananda

19. Blockly Games: Pond Tutor

What you will learn today:

- *Understand the basics of 'Pond' games.*
- *Use code block to shoot a target.*
- *Solve the same problem using JavaScript.*

The Pond Tutor introduces the concept of text-based programming using JavaScript along with block-based coding. For these games you can switch between blocks and actual JavaScript in editor.

JavaScript was not covered in this book. However, the examples of JavaScript that pops up at the end of each game will give you some idea about the nature of commands in JavaScript coding language.

This is an introduction of transition from block-based coding to more advanced practices.

Pond Tutor Level 1 and 2

Use the 'cannon' command to hit the target. The first parameter is the angle, the second parameter is the range. Find the right combination to hit the target.

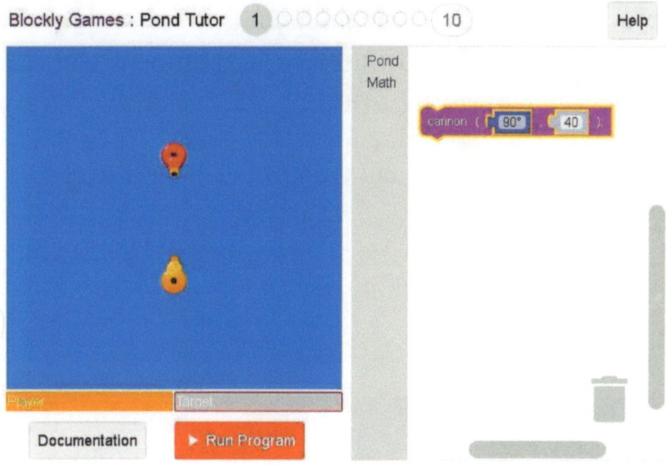

Fig. 19.1: Code for Pond Tutor Level 1

The Level 1 Pond uses block-based coding. Experiment with changing the angle and range to see the effect. Continue until the target is hit.

Fig. 19.2: JavaScript for Pond Tutor Level 2

The Level 3 Pond uses the same problem, but the command is to be given through the text-based interface. Experiment with changing the angle and range to see the effect.

Further on, you may experiment with Level 3 and Level 4.

In Level 3, the target needs to be hit many times. Use a 'while (true)' loop to do something indefinitely.

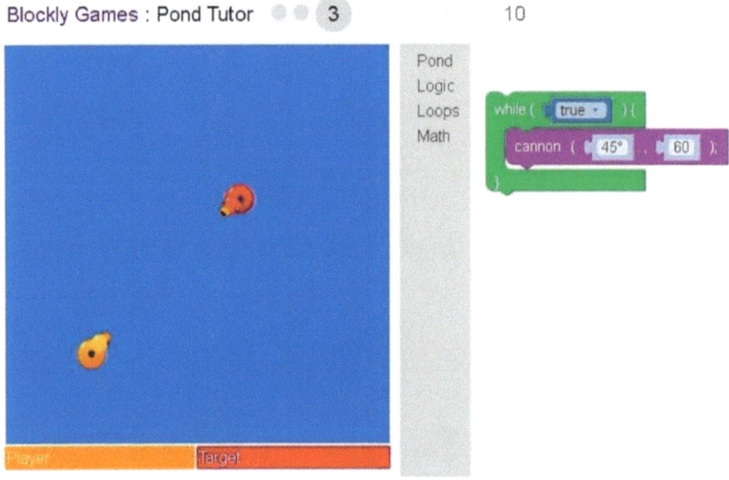

19.3: Pond tutor level 3

In Level 4, the target needs to be hit many times like that in Level3 by using command through JavaScript.

Watch the JavaScript command structure for 'while (true)' loop to do something indefinitely.

```
while (true) {
  cannon(270, 60);
}
```

20. Blockly Games: Pond

What you will learn today:

- *Understand the basics of 'Pond' games.*
- *Solve the same problem using JavaScript.*
- *Learn how complex application sums up learning from Blockly Games.*

The Pond in Blockly Games is a challenge to program an interesting game that you will love. However, at this stage you are expected to solve it yourself. Just use the codes given here and watch how the program works.

About the game

You can use either blocks or JavaScript. All your learning so far through the different game levels will be used in this level.

The Pond is a dangerous place. Everyone is firing. The Rook fires in all 8 directions, the Sniper fires when at a corner, the Counter fires when finds a target, and you the Player. Who wins???

The main goal of the pond is to eliminate the other ducks and win. Your strategy can be to run around, scan for the enemies, locate and shoot at them.

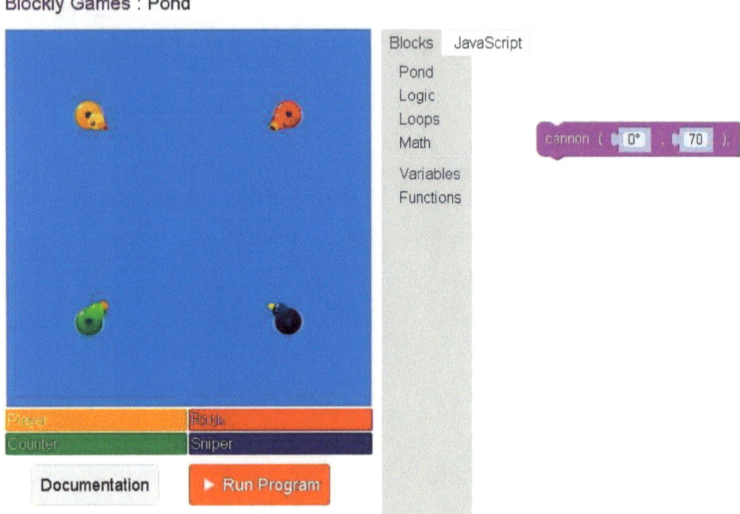

Fig. 20.1: The Pond Game

The enemies are the Rook, the Sniper and the Counter. Sniper shoots only when he gets to a corner. The Rook runs through the middle scanning in four directions. The Counters strategy is to find someone, then to stand still and shoot them.

For the brave ones I am proving only the solutions that you can attempt for one type of solution (Fig. 20.2).

Tasks

1. Simply construct code blocks as shown in Fig. 202.2 and run the program.

2. Type the JavaScript for the same program and run it.

These will give you a basic idea about further possibilities of coding.

If this makes you interested, you can learn JavaScript on your own!!!

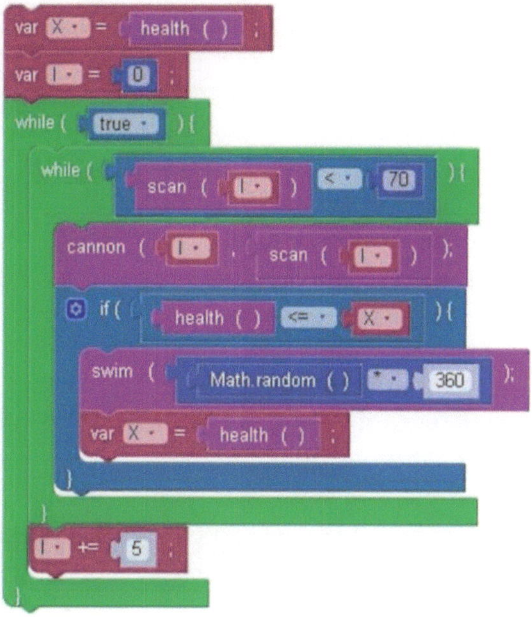

Fig. 20.2: Pond solution

JavaScript for the above code:

```javascript
var X, I;
X = health();
I = 0;
while (true) {
  while (scan(I) <= 70) {
    cannon(scan(I), I);
    if (health() <= X) {
      swim(Math.random() * 360);
      X = health();
    }
  }
  I += 5;
}
```

Blockly Games: Review

What you will learn today:

- *Recall the learning from Puzzle and Maze games.*
- *Review what is covered in Bird, Turtle games.*
- *Appreciate the more to learn from Music and Pond games.*

What have you done so far?

Blockly Games teaches you coding in various ways and steps. You started with assembling the code blocks for different type of animals. That was in the Puzzle games.

Then you helped a robot to navigate through different maze. It was interesting challenge through mazes of different levels of difficulty. In the process you learned the use of different types of codes or program structures like sequence, loops, decision blocks.

These are fundamental concepts used in any programming task. Developing solutions for maze problems also helped you in computational thinking and coding practice.

After Maze, you controlled a bird (drone) to get the worm and return to the nest through obstacles. Then you controlled a Turtle to make a drawing. Then you learned how to create shapes with mathematics.

After these were the Music, where you created music using the code blocks. In the Pond Tutor, all your learning is used. You have just experienced only four levels of this game. Applications of all these are used in the Pond battle!!

Epilogue

What you will learn today:

- *Review what have understood about learning to learn.*
- *Appreciate that all power is within you.*
- *Appreciate the power concentration and its need for students.*

Everyone will tell us to learn maths, science, literature and so on and so on. What is the process?

Learning to learn is a fundamental skill that you need to develop. You have proved your abilities after completing the exercises.

You must be feeling confident by solving the problems on your own. This experience will help you in learning to learn any subject. In turn, this will improve your computational thinking capability.

The experience in learning computational thinking through this book would be equally applicable in any subject area, be it science or literature, maths or biology, physics, or geography.

You may take guidance from experienced ones, from your teachers and elders. However, instead of entirely depending on others you should take initiative to learn and explore yourself.

Please continue to move forward and be a good human being. *"All power is within you; you can do anything and everything." – Swami Vivekananda.*

While concluding this book I also remembered one piece of advice from Swamiji, which I feel is very important for any student.

> *"If I had to do my education over again, and had any voice in the matter, I would not study facts at all. I would develop the power of concentration and detachment, and then with a perfect instrument, I Could collect facts at will."*

This practice of concentration is essential for any learner. It is particularly needed for developing computational thinking. So, practice concentration and then practice, practice and practice. These habits will surely help you achieve great things by realising your potential. Always remember, there are immense potential in you. You can do anything and everything if you set your mind to it.

In conclusion, code the Indian national anthem in Blockly music group with codes as shown in Fig.22.1, stand up and play.

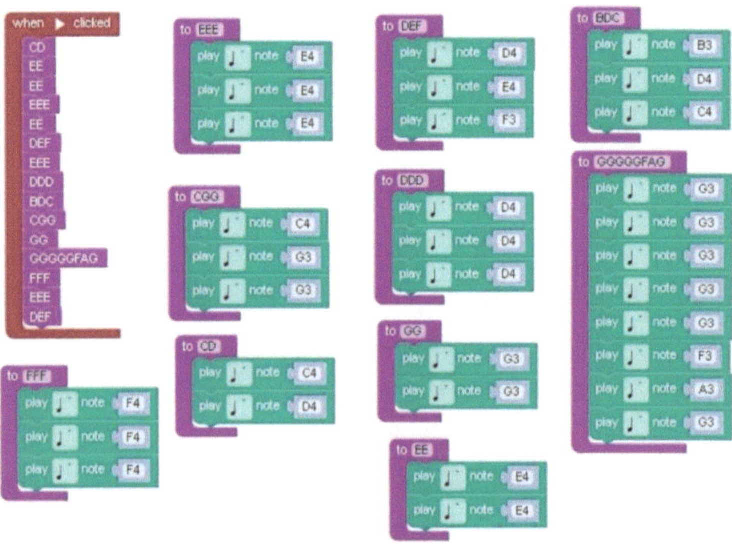

Fig. 22.1: Music Notes for National Anthem

Jana Gana Mana.	Adhi nayak Jaya Hey.
CD EE EE.	EEE EE DEF.
Bhaarat Bhaagya	Vidhata Punjab Sindh
EEE DDD BDC	CGG GG..
Gujarat Maratha	Draavid Utkal Banga
GGGG GFAG	FFF EEE DFE.
Vindhya Himachal	Yamuna Ganga.
EEE EED	GGG FF EE DD BDC

Appendix 1: Solutions for Bird 10 levels

In the Bird group of Blockly Games you can experiment with more conditionals and control flow. Here, the motion directions are expressed by angles and problems are explored with increasingly complex conditions.

Bird Level 1

Bird Level 2

Bird Level 3

Bird Level 4

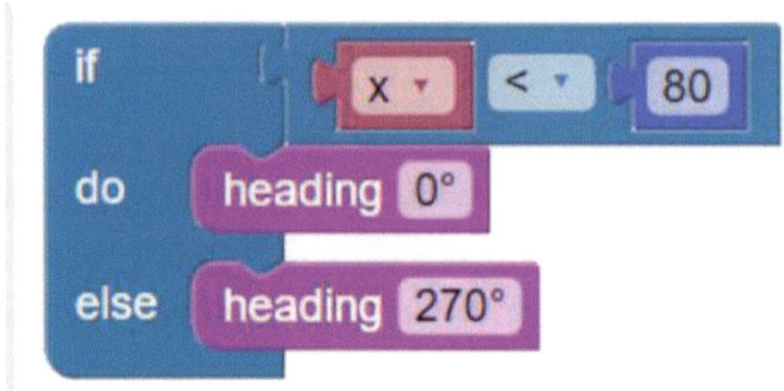

Bird Level 5

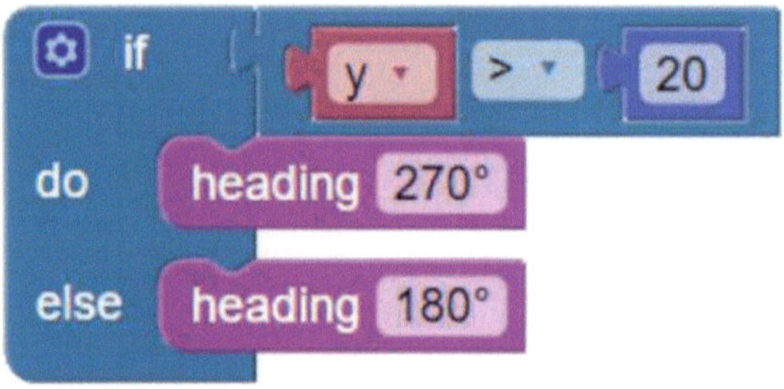

Bird Level 6

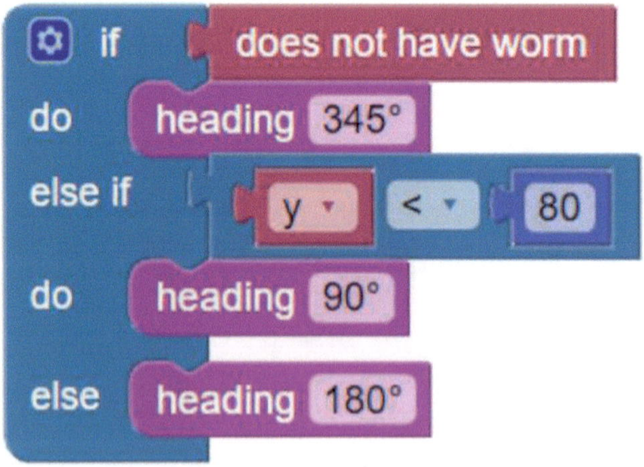

Bird Level 7

```
if      y ▾   > ▾   50
do      heading 225°
else if     does not have worm
do      heading 300°
else    heading 180°
```

Bird Level 8

```
if      y ▾   < ▾   40
do      heading 90°
else if     does not have worm
do      heading 345°
else if     x ▾  > ▾  50   and   y ▾  < ▾  50
do      heading 180°
else    heading 45°
```

Bird Level 9

```
if     does not have worm   and   [ x > 20 ]
do     heading 180°
else if  does not have worm   and   [ y > 20 ]
do     heading 270°
else if  [ y < 70 ]   and   [ x < 40 ]
do     heading 90°
else     heading 315°
```

Bird Level 10

```
if     does not have worm   and   [ y < 80 ]   and   [ x < 30 ]
do     heading 90°
else if  does not have worm   and   [ x < 80 ]
do     heading 0°
else if  does not have worm   and   [ y > 50 ]
do     heading 270°
else if  [ y < 80 ]   and   [ x > 20 ]
do     heading 90°
else if  [ x > 20 ]
do     heading 180°
else if  [ y > 20 ]
do     heading 270°
```

Appendix 2: Solutions for Turtle 10 levels

Turtle Level 1

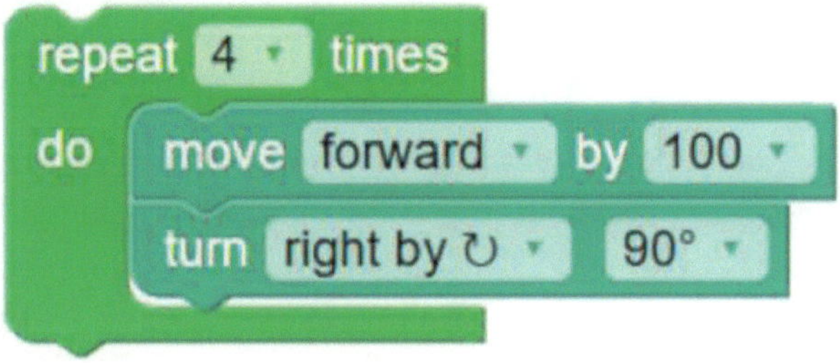

Turtle Level 2

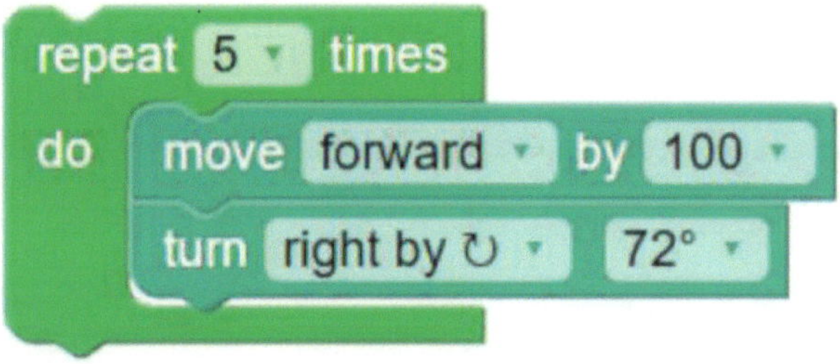

Turtle Level 3

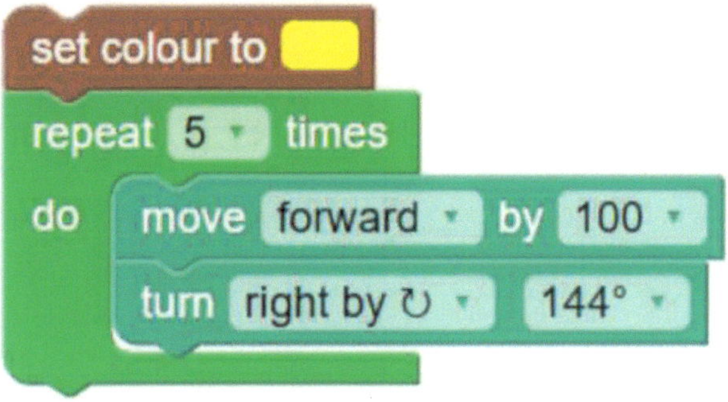

Turtle Level 4

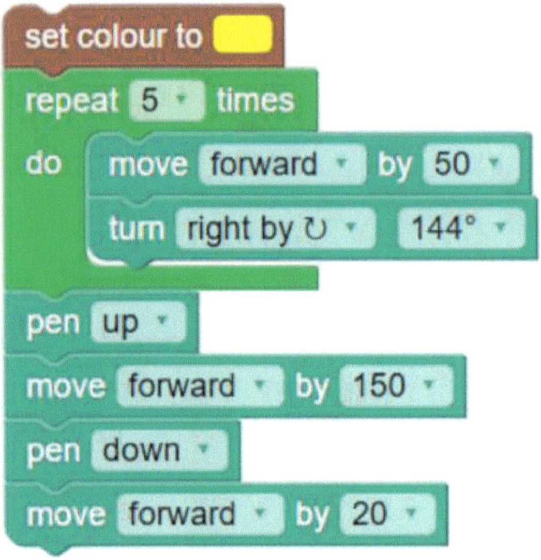

Turtle Level 5

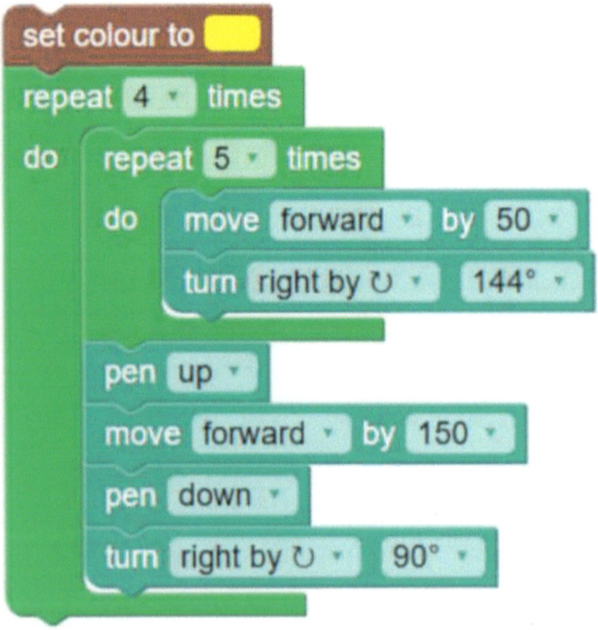

Turtle Level 6

```
set colour to [yellow]
repeat 3 times
do   repeat 5 times
     do   move forward by 50
          turn right by ↻ 144°

     pen up
     move forward by 150
     pen down
     turn right by ↻ 120°

set colour to [white]
pen up
turn right by ↻ 90°
turn right by ↻ 90°
turn right by ↻ 90°
move forward by 100
pen down
move forward by 50
```

Turtle level 7

```
set colour to [yellow]
repeat 3 times
do  repeat 5 times
    do  move forward by 50
        turn right by ↻ 144°

    pen up
    move forward by 150
    pen down
    turn right by ↻ 120°

turn left by ↺ 90°
pen up
set colour to [white]
move forward by 100
pen down
repeat 4 times
do  move forward by 50
    move backward by 50
    turn right by ↻ 45°
```

Turtle Level 8

```
set colour to [yellow]
repeat 3 times
do  repeat 5 times
    do  move forward by 50
        turn right by ↻ 144°
    pen up
    move forward by 150
    pen down
    turn right by ↻ 120°
turn left by ↺ 90°
pen up
set colour to [white]
move forward by 100
pen down
repeat 360 times
do  move forward by 50
    move backward by 50
    turn right by ↻ 1°
```

Turtle Level 9

Turtle Level10

About the book

The book is meant for anyone (from 8-108 years) who are interested to learn the 21st-century skill. Students will be able to take a deep dive into Computation Thinking and programming constructs through Blockly Games created by Google. The book will take you through a journey consisting of

- Guided lessons (Chapters 1 to 14)
- Semi guided lessons with exercises (Chapters 15 to 16)
- Exploratory lessons (Chapters 17 to 20)

About the author

Ashok Banerji, MTech, PhD, SMACM has a distinguished career in academics teaching educational technology, multimedia and computing at the University Teesside, Singapore Polytechnic, Jones International University and the University of Liverpool Online. He introduced many teachers to the wonderland of educational technology. His passion is teaching Computational Thinking and Scratch programming to children and authoring books for them. http://www.linkedin.com/in/ashokbanerji

Other books:

Available at Notion Press, Flipkart and Amazon:

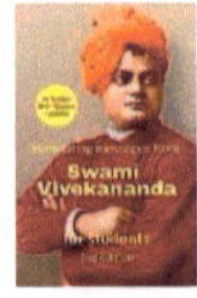

Stimulating Messages from Swami Vivekananda (2nd ed) ISBN: 979 888 923 9079:
https://notionpress.com/read/stimulating-messages-from-swami-vivekananda-2nd-ed

Saswata Bani (Eternal messages in Bengali) ISBN: 979 888 833 1583:
https://notionpress.com/read/saswata-bani

Computational Thinking with Blockly Games (Colour) ISBN: 979 889 026 047-5
https://notionpress.com/read/computational-thinking-with-blockly-games

Computational Thinking with Blockly Games (B&W version) a step-by-step guide for young learners ISBN: 979 889 026 103-8
https://notionpress.com/read/computational-thinking-with-blockly-games-b-w-version

Upcoming

Computational Thinking with Scratch unleashing creativity of the young

Computational Thinking with HTML exploring the mystery

www.ingramcontent.com/pod-product-compliance
Lightning Source LLC
Chambersburg PA
CBHW040854110726
48005CB00001B/55